Praise for
Still Learning: Strengthening Professional and Organizational Capacity

Still Learning focuses on strengthening social-emotional capacity among educators to help individuals, teams, and organizations do more good. But it's more than that—it's about how to live a better, richer life and make a difference in the lives of our colleagues and our children.

Allison understands the value of reflection, and she provides prompts throughout the book for readers to look back, look at, and look ahead to what's possible in our collective work. She also recognizes the impact of praxis, or real-life application, in professional learning and embeds tools within and beyond the book to guide meaningful action. I am a better person for having read this book, and I think you will be, too.

—**Dr. Jim Knight**, senior partner, Instructional Coaching Group and author of
The Definitive Guide to Instructional Coaching, The Impact Cycle, and *Better Conversations*

Allison Rodman understands teachers and educational organizations deeply. She challenges us to remember to take time to focus not only on our students' development, but on our own development as well. In *Still Learning*, Rodman wonderfully supports educators with research and reflective exercises that support us in that growth. Full of resources and information, this book will be a companion for so many as we challenge ourselves to stretch at our edges.

—**Jennifer Abrams**, author of *Having Hard Conversations* and
Stretching Your Learning Edges: Growing (Up) at Work

For many years, my mantra has been "There is no mountaintop to teaching," so I was anxious to explore what Allison Rodman offered educators in *Still Learning*. I found it packed with challenging questions, supporting research, strategies, suggestions, and insights to support educators individually and collectively. Schools can only focus on the whole child if they focus on the whole educator. Allison provides pathways to that purpose.

—**Steve Barkley**, chief learning officer, PLS3rdLearning and
author of *Instructional Coaching with the End in Mind*

In a field so often focused on nurturing others, *Still Learning: Strengthening Professional and Organizational Capacity* invites educators to prioritize themselves. This transformative work, a compass for personal and professional growth, boldly addresses a gap in education literature. Blending rich insights with actionable strategies, it pioneers a journey of self-discovery, focusing on social-emotional capacity. As the boundaries between personal and professional blur, this book is a lifeline. Its holistic approach, a response to escalating demands, nurtures educators' well-being. Through poignant reflections and research-based tools, it cultivates a resilient, empowered community of learners, essential for shaping the long game. Engage with this book—immerse, savor, and emerge stronger. For educators who commit their hearts and minds, this is the guide they deserve.

—**Jill Thompson**, partner, Education Elements

In *Still Learning*, Rodman masterfully provides opportunities and tools for educators to breathe life into the Whole School, Whole Community, Whole Child model through cultivating individual and organizational capacity. She brings to life research through practitioner perspectives to lead readers toward reflection and action in the interest of student success.

—**Dr. Hannah Gbenro**, chief academic officer, Washington State

WOW! Allison Rodman has written an incredible book based on research from the education field and beyond. Each chapter includes a high-level theory of change coupled with a practical and action-oriented how-to guide. She has a unique talent for making the abstract and complex feel concrete and accessible. Multiple times while reviewing this book, I thought of other leaders and how much they absolutely *needed* this resource. That, to me, is the measure of a must-read.

—**Dr. PJ Caposey**, Illinois Superintendent of the Year and
National Superintendent of the Year finalist

Allison Rodman's *Still Learning* takes an in-depth, thoughtful, and essential look at how educators must focus on their own learning, well-being, and emotional investment in education. Too often in education, we apply effective learning strategies for our students but ignore educators. We assume lifelong learning is a mindset to be instilled in our classrooms but not across staff or board rooms. This book dispels that myth and applies the same learning focus to adults—not just teachers, but anyone involved in the teaching and learning process, including board members, district and school leaders, counselors, support staff members, parents, and caregivers. *Still Learning* is essential reading for educators in all these groups and will help you reframe your own learning and growth.

Educators often find it difficult to make time to reflect on their own learning. We are fundamentally servant-leaders. Yet, as Rodman points out, this book provides time and space to engage in your own learning. Take the time to "[i]ndulge, preserve, recover. Take all the time you need to soak in its pages, process, and grow. We need you for the long game."

—**Sean Slade**, speaker and head of BTS Spark North America and author of *Questioning Education* and *School Climate Change*

Cultivating effective teams is complex work. With *Still Learning*, Rodman provides a thoughtful and comprehensive guide. She synthesizes a wide variety of expert thinking on adult learning needs, organizing it around the core issues that are essential for creating effective learning environments for both students and educators. This book is packed with resources and includes QR access to helpful materials. *Still Learning* is a valuable resource for anyone who wants to create and sustain effective teams.

—**Stefani Arzonetti Hite**, founder of Tigris Solutions and author of *Leading Collective Effective Efficacy* and *Intentional and Targeted Teaching*

Still Learning is a beacon that illuminates a crucial yet overlooked aspect of education: support for adult social-emotional learning (SEL). Too often, we ask educators to focus on fostering these essential skills without providing a practical framework grounded in recognizing the adults' need to develop and deepen their competency. Allison Rodman's skillful integration of SEL competencies and adult learning theory provides an exemplary framework for building and sustaining educators' professional growth. *Still Learning* is guaranteed to be a go-to guide for administrators, instructional coaches, and professional learning facilitators.

—**Dr. Krista Leh**, chief education officer, Resonance Educational Consulting

Still Learning is the book I wished I had written—and the book I needed to read! Allison Rodman has created an amazing and incredibly helpful resource to support educators' social and emotional learning needs. *Still Learning* incorporates so many elements of important and timeless frameworks—from SEL competencies to CliftonStrengths and chronotypes. Reading Allison's work has really helped me see where my growth and development as a human being sit in relation to my learning as an educator. Thank you, Allison, for finally connecting the dots and helping me see that, as an educator, learning about myself is as important as learning about my content.

—**Dr. Isabel Sawyer**, senior vice president, The Collaborative Classroom and author of *Professional Learning Redefined*

When choosing professional books to read, one can always count on the quality and value that Allison Rodman delivers. *Still Learning* is no exception. She gets to the heart of the research, shows application across multiple avenues, and shares the voices of others to amplify our profession. Get ready to grow and explore who you are as a professional so that you serve at the highest level. Lucky us!

—**LaVonna Roth**, keynote speaker, author, and consultant, Ignite Your S.H.I.N.E.®, Inc.

STILL
LEARNING

Also by Allison Rodman

Personalized Professional Learning:
A Job-Embedded Pathway for Elevating Teacher Voice

STILL LEARNING

Strengthening Professional and Organizational Capacity

ALLISON RODMAN

ascd

Arlington, Virginia USA

2800 Shirlington Road, Suite 1001 • Arlington, VA 22206 USA
Phone: 800-933-2723 or 703-578-9600 • Fax: 703-575-5400
Website: www.ascd.org • Email: member@ascd.org
Author guidelines: www.ascd.org/write

Richard Culatta, *Chief Executive Officer;* Anthony Rebora, *Chief Content Officer;* Genny Ostertag, *Managing Director, Book Acquisitions & Editing;* Mary Beth Nielsen, *Director, Book Editing;* Miriam Calderone, *Editor;* Thomas Lytle, *Creative Director;* Donald Ely, *Art Director;* Lisa Hill, *Graphic Designer;* Valerie Younkin, *Senior Production Designer;* Kelly Marshall, *Production Manager;* Shajuan Martin, *E-Publishing Specialist;* Christopher Logan, *Senior Production Specialist;* Kathryn Oliver, *Creative Project Manager*

Copyright © 2024 ASCD. All rights reserved. It is illegal to reproduce copies of this work in print or electronic format (including reproductions displayed on a secure intranet or stored in a retrieval system or other electronic storage device from which copies can be made or displayed) without the prior written permission of the publisher. By purchasing only authorized electronic or print editions and not participating in or encouraging piracy of copyrighted materials, you support the rights of authors and publishers. Readers who wish to reproduce or republish excerpts of this work in print or electronic format may do so for a small fee by contacting the Copyright Clearance Center (CCC), 222 Rosewood Dr., Danvers, MA 01923, USA (phone: 978-750-8400; fax: 978-646-8600; web: www.copyright.com). To inquire about site licensing options or any other reuse, contact ASCD Permissions at www.ascd.org/permissions or permissions@ascd.org. For a list of vendors authorized to license ASCD ebooks to institutions, see www.ascd.org/epubs. Send translation inquiries to translations@ascd.org.

ASCD® is a registered trademark of Association for Supervision and Curriculum Development. All other trademarks contained in this book are the property of, and reserved by, their respective owners, and are used for editorial and informational purposes only. No such use should be construed to imply sponsorship or endorsement of the book by the respective owners.

All web links in this book are correct as of the publication date below but may have become inactive or otherwise modified since that time. If you notice a deactivated or changed link, please email books@ascd.org with the words "Link Update" in the subject line. In your message, please specify the web link, the book title, and the page number on which the link appears.

PAPERBACK ISBN: 978-1-4166-3239-9   ASCD product #121034   n11/23

PDF EBOOK ISBN: 978-1-4166-3240-5; see Books in Print for other formats.

Quantity discounts are available: email programteam@ascd.org or call 800-933-2723, ext. 5773, or 703-575-5773. For desk copies, go to www.ascd.org/deskcopy.

Library of Congress Cataloging-in-Publication Data
Names: Rodman, Allison (Allison M.), author.
Title: Still learning: strengthening professional and organizational capacity / Allison Rodman.
Description: Arlington, VA : ASCD, 2024. | Includes bibliographical references and index.
Identifiers: LCCN 2023028359 (print) | LCCN 2023028360 (ebook) | ISBN 9781416632399 (paperback) | ISBN 9781416632405 (pdf)
Subjects: LCSH: Professional learning communities. | Educators—Professional relationships.
Classification: LCC LB1731 .R59 2024 (print) | LCC LB1731 (ebook) | DDC 371.1—dc23/eng/20230714
LC record available at https://lccn.loc.gov/2023028359
LC ebook record available at https://lccn.loc.gov/2023028360

33 32 31 30 29 28 27 26 25 24   1 2 3 4 5 6 7 8 9 10 11 12

"There is no passion to be found in playing small—
in settling for a life that is less than the one you are capable of living."
Nelson Mandela

To all the learners who model the way for others—
board members, district and school leaders, teachers,
counselors, support staff members, parents, and caregivers—
may this book strengthen your capacity to keep learning and growing.

STILL LEARNING

Strengthening Professional and Organizational Capacity

ACKNOWLEDGMENTS

This book—true to its title—provides a quintessential example of what it means to be *still learning*. The initial outline was drafted in fall 2019, the book was contracted in summer 2020...and, well, we all continued to learn together. I wrote and rewrote, the research expanded, the profession evolved, and I rewrote again. The text shifted. We all shifted...and grew. And I worked relentlessly to keep pace with the changing landscape and educators' developing needs. I committed to honoring our present reality, while also pushing the boundaries of where we have the potential to evolve as a field. Through it all, it was the people in my network—not the programs, processes, or policies—who provided support, thought partnership, and a reminder of what's possible.

I am forever grateful to Monica Burns, Krista Leh, and Tammy Musiowsky-Borneman. As we canceled speaking and consulting engagements from our calendars one by one, beginning in March 2020, it was this group of exceptional professionals who leaned in and embraced our collective opportunity for learning. We took courses together—both inside and outside the education field—to hone our craft and better serve our partners in even more intentional and personalized ways. We consistently showed up for one another and operated from a place of abundance, recognizing that we grew stronger together. We didn't feel the term *mastermind* quite fit our collaborative approach—though in structure that's what it was—and we referred to our collective as our Pineapple Pod. My kids continue to make fun of us and the "pod" time that gets blocked on my calendar, but I won't apologize for it. It defines us. We committed to draw others in and continue learning at a time when so many felt isolated—and we continue to do so.

Chapters 3 and 4 speak directly to the power of vulnerability. The reciprocal relationship I've come to share and deeply appreciate with ASCD's managing director of Book Acquisitions and Editing, Genny Ostertag, is a model of transparency and constant learning. I love to read and process content in a format that is beneficial for practitioners on the ground. I seek to produce the kinds of books, articles, and tools I needed as an instructional coach and a school leader. Although I am a solid writer, I am a painfully slow one. I deliberate over every word, and as a constant learner, I am quite possibly every editor's worst nightmare. Genny not only accepts my idiosyncrasies as a writer, but also is incredibly transparent about her own growth opportunities, and she continuously shares insights from the field. We keep learning together, and I deeply value the guidance she provides.

The working relationship with my content editor, Miriam Calderone, is a model of what I hope for the education profession at this moment. Together, we expanded the notion of what education books typically look like. We asked, "What if?" more times than I can count. "What if there were more links and QR codes? What if it was all downloadable and editable? What if the tools were stored in a space we could consistently update as the work continued to evolve? What if there were more tools than what existed in the print book? What if we simultaneously wrote and built for both individual educators and system leaders?" The volume of moving parts, intricacy of detail, and level of precision to compile the figures, resources, links, and tools in this manuscript were, by definition, next level. As a practitioner at heart, I appreciated the value of these components, and Miriam met me every step of the way. She pushed boundaries where we could and provided clear guidance when we couldn't. Every image, icon, and insane idea I conjured up, she helped bring to the printing press. I am truly grateful for her patience, attention to detail, and commitment to learning—for all of us.

Finally, thank you to my family. I could not write about constant learning if I weren't surrounded by it every day. Throughout the development of this book, my husband, Doug, facilitated learning for his students whose scores exceeded Advanced Placement global averages. Our son, Cameron, won a soccer state championship. Our daughter Aislinn won an archery national championship. And our daughter Lola consistently reminded all of us of the importance of embracing new experiences every single day and being unapologetic in our own skin. From the classroom to the field to all the spaces in between, my family centered me and enabled me to be present while also giving me space to learn and grow. I love you.

INTRODUCTION

Whatever the reasons, we do not pursue emotional development with the same intensity with which we pursue physical and intellectual development. This is all the more unfortunate because full emotional development offers the greatest degree of leverage in attaining our full potential.

—William O'Brien

This may be one of the first education books you read—though I certainly hope it is not the last—focused on adults rather than children. It is a work centered on identity, goal orientation, capacity strengthening, and community tending in a way not previously explored. Some may see it as self-indulgent in a field so firmly focused on service; others may see it as supporting self-preservation in a profession marked by burnout. Either way, this book is for you. Indulge, preserve, recover. Take all the time you need to soak in its pages, process, and grow. We need you for the long game.

Our Collective Need

My first book, *Personalized Professional Learning: A Job-Embedded Pathway for Elevating Teacher Voice* (2019), sparked conversations about the need to place greater emphasis on andragogy, or adult learning, in parallel to schools' focus on pedagogy and curriculum. The idea for this book formed shortly after my first book was published, as readers responded to the text and I continued to see adult learning shifting, evolving, and, in some ways, remaining the same or even moving backward. So, I drafted an outline about our collective need to strengthen educators' social-emotional capacity alongside their content mastery and skill development. Many of the educators I've supported struggled with their own self-awareness and self-management challenges (myself included at times), especially as education continues to become an ever-more demanding field, so it seems unfair to look to them as social-emotional models for students without also helping them grow their own social-emotional learning. I wanted to share reflections, tools, and strategies both to strengthen educators' own social-emotional capacity and to better equip them to support students.

Little did I know when I compiled that first outline where we would be at the time of publication. To say the need for this work has escalated is an understatement. The boundaries between educators' professional and personal lives are blurred now more than ever before, yet we continue to focus training and workshops almost exclusively on instruction while other fields offer professional learning centered on self-growth (e.g., on such topics as goal setting, prioritization and time management, and collaboration) as much as, if not more than, content expertise and strategy.

Systems of Support—For Students

We saw a shift toward systemwide capacity building and professional learning centered on students' social-emotional needs as we transitioned back to in-school learning following the closures due to COVID-19 and sought to reacclimate students to social norms. The longer we operated outside the traditional model we had come to understand as "school," the greater the perceived need for social-emotional supports (though such needs have long existed). It is somewhat ironic that we had to remove our social connections—at least those that were place-based—to fully grasp the impact of social-emotional wellness on learning and development.

Whole School, Whole Community, Whole Child

Though it may have taken a global pandemic for social-emotional learning (SEL) to find its necessary place in both educator practice and professional learning, frameworks to support SEL have undergone several cycles of development and refinement over the past 25 years. In 1997, ASCD published *Promoting Social and Emotional Learning: Guidelines for Educators*—the first major work to define and describe social-emotional learning, authored by members of the Research and Guidelines Work Group of the Collaborative for Academic, Social, and Emotional Learning (CASEL). This text and its iterations continue to guide social-emotional learning at the state, district, and school levels today.

In 2006, ASCD convened the Commission on the Whole Child, a cross-section of business and education leaders that published *The Learning Compact Redefined: A Call to Action*. In this report, the commission noted that the "current educational practice and policy focus is overwhelmingly on academic achievement. This achievement, however, is but one element of student learning and development and only a part of any complete system of educational accountability" (Bramante et al., 2007, p. 3). In 2010, the whole child tenets—students who are healthy, safe, engaged, supported, and challenged—were further defined across 50 indicators, and in 2012 ASCD partnered with the Centers for Disease Control and Prevention (CDC) to develop the Whole School, Whole Community, Whole Child (or WSCC) model (see Figure I.1). This model recognizes the need for education, public health, and school health sectors to become better aligned and collaborate to improve each child's cognitive, physical, social, and emotional development. Twenty-eight states have written "whole child" into their Every Student Succeeds Act consolidated state plans, and 13 states have written the WSCC Model directly into their plans (Slade, 2020).

Together, ASCD and the CDC identified 10 components for coordinating policy, process, and practice and improving both learning and health. Among these components is employee wellness. "Fostering the physical and mental health of school employees protects school staff and, by doing so, helps support students' health and academic success," notes the CDC

(2020, para. 5). "Healthy school employees are more productive and less likely to be absent." While the WSCC model highlights employee wellness as an essential component for supporting the whole child, attention almost exclusively centers on elements of physical health such as healthy eating, active lifestyles, abstaining from tobacco, and avoiding injury and exposure to hazards. Stress and depression receive mention but are not emphasized as much as physical health.

FIGURE I.1
The Whole School, Whole Community, Whole Child (WSCC) Model

Source: Centers for Disease Control and Prevention and ASCD. *Whole School, Whole Community, Whole Child (WSCC) model.* © 2012 ASCD.

SEL Competencies

Additional work must be done to build the social-emotional capacities of leaders, teachers, and other adults across our educational systems. Following the collaboration with ASCD, CASEL identified five SEL competencies to guide and assess the effectiveness of SEL programs at the state, district, and school levels. The competencies were originally published in 2012, and the complete "CASEL 5" framework (shown in Figure I.2) was updated in 2020. CASEL's five competencies are as follows:

Self-awareness: The abilities to understand one's own emotions, thoughts, and values and how they influence behavior across contexts...capacities to recognize one's strengths and limitations with a well-grounded sense of confidence and purpose.

Self-management: The abilities to manage one's emotions, thoughts, and behaviors effectively in different situations and to achieve goals and aspirations...the capacities to delay gratification, manage stress, and feel motivation and agency to accomplish personal and collective goals.

Social awareness: The abilities to understand the perspectives of and empathize with others, including those from diverse backgrounds, cultures, and contexts...the capacities to feel compassion for others, understand broader historical and social norms for behavior in different settings, and recognize family, school, and community resources and supports.

Relationship skills: The abilities to establish and maintain healthy and supportive relationships and to effectively navigate settings with diverse individuals and groups...the capacities to communicate clearly, listen actively, cooperate, work collaboratively to problem solve and negotiate conflict constructively, navigate settings with differing social and cultural demands and opportunities, provide leadership, and seek or offer help when needed.

Responsible decision-making: The abilities to make caring and constructive choices about personal behavior and social interactions across diverse situations...the capacities to consider ethical standards and safety concerns, and to evaluate the benefits and consequences of various actions for personal, social, and collective well-being. (CASEL, 2020b)

As of March 2020, CASEL had found that 18 states had developed K–12 SEL standards or competencies, with 12 utilizing the CASEL 5 framework and the rest using a state-specific SEL model. Of these 18, 6 reference the whole child and 13 include professional learning (CASEL 2020a, p. 5).

FIGURE I.2
The CASEL SEL Framework

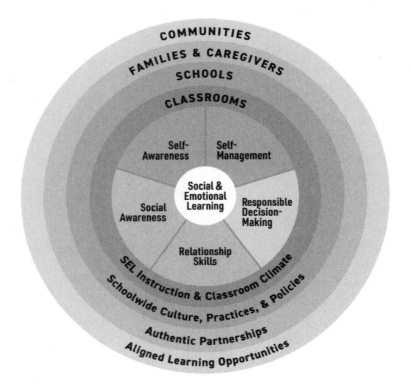

Source: From the Collaborative for Academic, Social, and Emotional Learning. Used with permission. © 2020b CASEL.

Despite this progress, a lack of attention to adult SEL remains an obstacle to effective implementation of SEL for students. CASEL's Collaborating Districts Initiative found that "schools are more effective at teaching and reinforcing SEL for students when they also cultivate SEL competencies in adults. Successful SEL implementation depends on how well staff work together to facilitate SEL instruction, foster a positive school community, and model social and emotional competence. This calls on schools to focus on adults' professional growth as educators as well as their own social and emotional learning" (CASEL, n.d.). In a brief report on lessons learned from district leaders who had been implementing SEL since 2011, CASEL highlights this need in greater detail:

> While each [district leader] offered unique insights about how they would do things differently if they all started over, they all had one common lesson: We should have focused more on the adults in the beginning. Time and time again, districts said they mistakenly focused entirely on building the social and emotional competence of students without also considering the SEL needs of adults who are engaging with students every day. In order to create conditions for students to effectively engage in SEL, adults themselves need to feel empowered, supported, and valued. This calls on districts to foster a supportive staff community and promote adults' own SEL. (CASEL, 2019, p. 1)

The report goes on to highlight the importance of strengthening central office expertise; providing high-quality professional learning for schools; deepening adult social, emotional, and cultural competence; and building staff trust, community, and collective efficacy.

Further Evidence of Need

The need to tend to adult SEL emerges across research bases. In 2019, the Aspen Institute National Commission on Social, Emotional, and Academic Development (Aspen Commission) published a landmark two-year study titled *From a Nation at Risk to a Nation at Hope*. "Too often," the study reports, "teachers and school leaders do not receive preparation and ongoing learning that address the science of human development and how to translate that science into their practice. Teachers, in particular, must understand this work, own it, and help shape it. 'We have to start with adults' social and emotional learning, and then work on kids' social and emotional learning,' said a 4th grade teacher in Seattle" (p. 25).

Newer performance-based teacher preparation assessment systems require prospective teachers to attend to SEL by detailing how their understanding of their students' social, emotional, and cognitive development guides their lesson design, selection of materials and activities, and provided supports. In years past, similar performance assessments typically included elements of differentiated instruction (e.g., process, product, content, and environment) but did not directly address students' social-emotional needs.

More than 600 educator preparation programs in 40 states and the District of Columbia currently use the Educative Teacher Performance Assessment (edTPA), a preparation program developed by the Stanford Center for Assessment, Learning, and Equity (SCALE), as a preservice assessment, and at least 18 states have or are considering such an assessment for teacher licensure or certification (Aspen Commission, 2019). However, this assessment does not evaluate preservice teachers' social-emotional capacity to respond to an ever-changing environment with evolving student needs.

Dr. Stephanie Jones of Harvard's Graduate School of Education is the director of the school's Ecological Approaches to Social-Emotional Learning (EASEL) Laboratory, which explores the effects of high-quality social-emotional interventions. "It is difficult for adults to help students build these skills if they themselves do not possess them," Jones writes. "Research indicates that teachers with stronger social and emotional skills have more positive relationships with students, engage in more effective classroom management, and implement their students' social and emotional programming more effectively. Critically, not only teachers but district administrators, principals, and other school staff need professional training and support in social and emotional development and related practices" (Jones & Kahn, 2017–2018, pp. 20–21).

The American Institutes for Research reviewed 136 social-emotional frameworks and found that "many frameworks mention youth, children, or adolescence but do not necessarily provide relevant age ranges. . . . Eleven frameworks refer to *school-age* child, 19 refer to *children,* 11 refer to *youth*, and three refer to *teens*. A total of 32 refer to *adolescents* as a primary age group of interest, often in combination with either children or young adults. The term *adults* appears 10 times across frameworks" (Berg et al., 2017, p. 37). Although research indicates that personal and social transitions require individuals to develop and refine *new* social-emotional competencies over time (Hair et al., 2002), existing frameworks do not necessarily reflect this reality.

Closing the Gap—For Adults

This book builds upon current research in social-emotional learning both inside and outside education, exploring the disciplines of attunement, alignment, perspective, collective efficacy, and organizational learning through an andragogical lens and in both theoretical and practical terms. It provides educators with opportunities to pause and reflect as well as anchor their next steps using research-based strategies coupled with adult learners' experiences from the field. Collectively, the strategies, insights, reflections, and integration guides in this book offer a framework for creating and sustaining learning organizations where both students *and* educators can truly thrive.

The Framework for Educator Capacity Building (see Figure I.3) sequences, defines, and outlines the key concepts for each of the disciplines listed above. The framework references related adult learning theories as well as complementary SEL competencies from CASEL. In addition, each chapter in this book has a corresponding appendix containing an integration guide and a capacity-building plan to support individual and organizational implementation and meet the needs of a holistic learning organization from both an intrapersonal and an ecological perspective.

A Note on Capacity Building, Disciplines, and Organizations

The United Nations (n.d.) defines *capacity building* as "the process of developing and strengthening the skills, instincts, abilities, processes and resources that organizations and communities need to survive, adapt, and thrive in a fast-changing world," noting that an "essential ingredient in capacity-building is transformation that is generated and sustained over time from within; transformation of this kind goes beyond performing tasks to changing mindsets and attitudes" (para. 1). Some individuals view this type of professional growth as life skills development; others see it as social-emotional learning. Regardless of the term used, we know from the high numbers of educators leaving the field that stronger and more personalized capacity strengthening is needed for our districts and schools to survive, adapt, and thrive.

FIGURE I.3

Framework for Educator Capacity Building

	Attunement	Alignment	Perspective	Collective Efficacy	Organizational Learning
Discipline	Harmony between perceived self and presented self	Congruence between purpose and practice	*Organizationally:* Safety, belonging, and vulnerability that lead to connected learning community *Individually:* Shift in schema and reflection that leads to integrated change in behavior	Focus on continuous growth to become a deliberately developmental organization	Sustained commitment to evolve and thrive as a learning ecosystem
	Self		*Team*		*System*
Key Concepts	• Identity • Drive • Growth Profile	• Goals • Structured Time • Disciplined Action • Cadence of Accountability	• Safety • Belonging • Vulnerability • Shift in Schema • Space for Reflection	• Shared Vulnerability • Demonstrated Strength • Growth Mindset • Unifying Focus	• Technical Problems, Adaptive Challenges, and Generative Opportunities • Core Competencies of Learning Organizations • Growth-Oriented Ecosystem
Related Adult Learning Theory	Experiential Learning Theory (ELT)	Self-Directed Learning (SDL)	Transformational Learning (TL)	Adult Professional Culture (APC)	Action Reflection Learning (ARL)
Complementary CASEL SEL Competency	Self-Awareness	Self-Management	Social Awareness	Relationship Skills	Responsible Decision Making

I selected the term *discipline* quite intentionally to frame the key concepts of attunement, alignment, perspective, collective efficacy, and organizational learning in this book. I have positioned these disciplines as access points rather than pathways with a target proficiency level; the point of entry will be different for each educator (and, most likely, each discipline). While the disciplines can (and should) be developed individually, they also build upon and support one another. In fact, in reviewing practitioner contributions for this work, it became challenging at times to identify the point of best fit for some insights given the integrated nature of these concepts.

Unlike a *standard, competency,* or *skill,* we can never fully master a *discipline.* Instead, we consistently build our capacity to better understand and focus ourselves and to engage more meaningfully with others. As Howard Gardner (2006) notes, "A discipline constitutes a distinctive way of thinking about the world.... [There are] two meanings of discipline: mastery of a craft, and the capacity to renew that craft through regular application over the years" (pp. 26, 43). For adult learners, capacity building requires more than checking off a list of signature practices and related strategies. We must commit to consistently reconsidering and refining our understanding of ourselves and the ways in which this understanding impacts our work with others.

Throughout the book, you will see the term *organization* where you might typically expect to see *school* or *district.* One of my goals when developing this book was to make it accessible to as many educators as possible, regardless of position or school type. The term *organization* applies not only to schools or districts but also to grade-level or content-area teams, grade bands, and education-focused nonprofit or for-profit entities. Regardless of whether you hold a formal leadership position in any of these, this book offers a variety of opportunities for you to strengthen both your individual and organizational capacity.

Reflections

I highly encourage you to make time and space for the reflections included in each chapter and to revisit them at different points in your career, particularly as you transition from one position or school community to another. I distinctly note both *time* and *space* here because it is not uncommon for us to designate time on our calendars for professional learning activities without really committing to them and ensuring we're in the right headspace to fully engage, focus, and reflect. We may complete the exercises when we are tired, unfocused, or multitasking. To gain the full benefit of these reflections (as well as of the strategies and implementation guides) requires a commitment of both time *and* space.

If you feel stretched or stressed, complete your reflections in sections, turn them into bulleted lists, or integrate components one at a time into a daily journal. As someone deeply committed to productivity and efficiency, I can assure you that there is great value in deep thinking, intentional pausing, and clear processing free from the distractions that often cloud our profession. Take your time with this piece; consider it a journey to be experienced rather than a task to be completed.

If you are in a leadership position, use the reflections from this book as growth opportunities for your teams. Engage with them yourself first, modeling your commitment to the work both inwardly and outwardly. But after that, share—*always* share. This piece is meant to be a tool for collective efficacy and organizational learning as much as for personal growth.

Throughout the book, you will see four icons indicating opportunities for reflection, integration, and extension:

❚❚ The pause icon highlights moments for you to slow down and thoughtfully consider and respond to "Pause and Reflect" prompts.

🍃 The leaf icon indicates "Cultivate Your Capacity" learning opportunities, which focus on strengthening individual capacity.

🌳 The tree icon signals "Cultivate Organizational Capacity" integration activities, which focus on strengthening your broader organization's capacity—whether that is your team, school, or system.

🔁 The loop icon features "Extend the Learning Loop" sections, which provide resources for additional exploration and deeper learning.

In addition, a QR code provided in each chapter enables you to access editable PDF versions of many of the reflection and action-planning tools within this book. I hope these will support and enhance your reflection, learning, and action planning. Readers can also access all the resources via the QR code on this page or by visiting https://www.thelearningloop.com/still-learning and navigating to the page for each discipline. For readers, all downloads are provided free of charge using the case-sensitive password "StillLearning."

Insights

I took extensive care to collect insights from teachers, coaches, leaders, and educational service providers across a variety of organizational types (public, private, charter, independent, nonprofit, for-profit, government), sizes, geographic locations, races, genders, and positions. Having served in a number of the represented positions myself, I understand the importance of seeing yourself in the work rather than viewing concepts through the lens of an outsider. I remain, now and always, a practitioner at heart, committed to a long-term vision of our holistic educational ecosystem as well as to an understanding of the day-to-day implications for those doing the work on the ground.

I leaned heavily on my professional learning network in writing this book, and they responded in kind to ensure the most representative picture possible. In these pages, you will find voices of individuals far more experienced than myself; I am humbled that they shared their personal insights and critical learnings with me. While I fully acknowledge that not all readers will find themselves in every contribution, my sincere hope in crafting this work is that you find yourself in at least one and are driven to connect, push deeper, and grow.

Strategies

The strategies outlined in each chapter are just that—strategies. Recognizing the extreme demands on educators' time, I attempted, as much as possible, to distill key findings from critical works to the most salient and applicable actions possible. They *are not* intended to constitute an all-encompassing program or exhaustive checklist; they *are* positioned to help educators transition reflections from thought to action and provide a scope of possibilities for what this work has the potential to look like in practice.

Please do not confuse these strategies with development targets or evaluative indicators. Doing so diminishes extremely challenging work to a set of checkboxes, columns, and rows. That is in no way the intended application of these strategies. Rather, use them as guideposts as you continue to learn side-by-side with your students.

Integration Guides and Capacity-Building Plans

As mentioned previously, each chapter has a corresponding appendix that includes an integration guide and a capacity-building plan to move you from understanding to reflection to action. Synthesizing key findings, and even helping readers find their own position within such findings, lacks value unless it points readers toward growth. The integration guides and capacity-building plans will help you consider which actions might best inform your practice. As noted earlier, the disciplines in this book are intended to be viewed as a continuous journey rather than a set of skills to be mastered. My hope is that you continually revisit this work, each time with new perspectives, lenses, and experiences to enhance its richness and implications for your own practice.

And Yes, Students

As an educator writing for educators, I would be remiss not to mention our students directly—how they inspire, motivate, and reenergize us, even years after they've left our classroom. Let's be honest, our students are our "why." They get us out of bed in the morning; they keep us awake at night. At its core, education is both "head" work *and* "heart" work. But for once—yes, just once—I am giving you permission for this to be about you—in the service of our students. Indulge, preserve, recover—but whatever you do, keep yourself in the game. We—they—need you.

1

ATTUNEMENT

Happiness is when what you think, what you say,
and what you do are in harmony.

—Mahatma Gandhi

Attunement Versus Balance

attune (verb): to bring into accord, harmony, or sympathetic relationship

The case for "balance" abounds in professional circles. A search for the term on the *Harvard Business Review* website returns close to 17,000 results. To many adults, balance is a utopian construct, often longed for but rarely achieved. Upon further examination, however, the idea of balance is just that—an idea, an illusion. Within the sequence and patterns of our daily decision making, we are always giving something up. As a working parent, if I spend extra time playing with my kids, I may be ordering takeout for dinner. If I make time to go to the gym, I may be late on a deadline. If I choose to attend a networking event, I may miss a kid's game or concert. I have made the difficult decisions to walk out of meetings, skip parades, and miss art shows and games. (And yes, I have sent in store-bought cookies for the class party.)

When exploring the discipline of attunement as adults, we must recognize the components of our identities, motivations, tendencies, and strengths that drive our daily decision-making processes. These decisions involve give and take, push and pull, back and forth. We do not balance them; we are always letting something go. As it relates to our social-emotional growth, the discipline of attunement is not about balancing but, instead, understanding (and coming to peace with) what we are letting go and why. Attunement is about coming to know ourselves and finding harmony among our thoughts, words, and actions; between our perceived self and our presented self.

To develop our attunement, we must first understand our identity, drive, and growth profile. We must discern *who we are, what motivates us,* and *how we learn and evolve* (see Figure 1.1). Once we do that, we can begin the work of attuning our inward and outward selves. As adults, we need to move beyond being self-aware and instead strive for a state of self-harmony where we bring our strongest personal and professional selves to the world.

FIGURE 1.1

Capacity-Building Blueprint: Attunement

Harmony Between Perceived Self and Presented Self		
Perceived Self	**=**	**Presented Self**
Identity Who we are	**Self-Harmony**	**Learning Professional**
Drive What motivates us		
Growth Profile How we learn and evolve		

As you read this chapter, you can use the QR code or visit https://www
.thelearningloop.com/book-attunement to access editable PDF versions
of the reflection and planning tools included throughout the text. Use
the case-sensitive password "StillLearning" to download the resources.

Identity

We develop the concept of identity at a young age, even before we can walk or
speak. We learn our mother's voice, our skin color, our preference for places
of calm or chaos. Some children display an affinity for movement, others
for smell, taste, or touch. It is not uncommon for preschool assignments to
ask children to identify favorite colors, foods, and leisure activities through
images before they can read. Collectively, over time, our circumstances and
choices come together to form our identity. As we grow into adolescents
and adults, the components of our identities are further complicated as we
navigate additional layers of selfhood and face more challenges related to
relationship building, personality conflict, and problem resolution. "Identity is not a static entity...," write Fadjukoff and colleagues (2016). "Instead,
changing life circumstances, together with changing biological and psychological needs, trigger further development during the decades of adult life"
(p. 8). We begin to see ourselves as larks or night owls, starters or finishers,
type A or B, fixed- or growth-minded. We learn to recognize our membership in multiple societal groups, and that our "home" culture may or may not
align with dominant culture, language, or historical context.

   Although identity plays a significant role in how we understand, process, and respond to our world, particularly as adults, it is not notably present in many existing SEL frameworks. Harvard's EASEL Lab engaged in a

taxonomy project titled "Explore SEL" to create a scientifically grounded system for organizing, describing, and connecting frameworks and skills across the nonacademic domain. The project sought to "create greater precision and transparency in the field of SEL and facilitate more effective translation between research and practice" (Jones et al., 2018). The Lab defines identity in this way:

> Identity encompasses how you understand and perceive yourself and your abilities. It includes your knowledge and beliefs about yourself, including your ability to learn and grow. When you feel good about yourself; sure of your place in the world; and confident in your ability to learn, grow, and overcome obstacles, it becomes easier to cope with challenges and build positive relationships.

In their review of 40 social-emotional frameworks across the six social-emotional domains of cognitive, emotion, social, values, perspectives, and identity, they found that only 10 frameworks (or 25 percent) emphasized the domain of identity more than 10 percent within the broader framework in relation to the other five domains, and that in eight of the frameworks, identity was not included at all (Jones et al., 2018). When tending to adults' social-emotional growth, the concept of identity cannot be overlooked.

Identity affects the way we interact with others, the decisions we make, and the subsequent actions we take. According to Fadjukoff (2016), "a meta-analysis covering 124 identity studies [by] Kroger, Martinussen, and Marcia (2010) concluded that it was not until age 36 that almost half of participants had reached overall identity achievement. Empirical research on identity formation in adulthood has highlighted that identity continues to develop during adult years for many people (e.g., Cramer, 2004; Josselson, 1996)" (p. 9). Social-emotional capacity building for adults requires that we understand ourselves not only in the past and present, but also as continuously evolving beings. Life experiences (both time-bound and circumstantial) affect how we perceive and present ourselves to the world.

In my conversations with educators, many have openly shared that, when tending to social-emotional growth, they tend to dive directly into goal setting and action planning without first considering who they truly are as individuals.

Pause and Reflect

Pause here to reflect on and respond to the identity prompts in Figure 1.2. You can either complete each of these social-emotional growth reflections in one sitting or separate the questions across multiple days as journal prompts. In either case, be sure you are giving yourself ample time and space to thoughtfully consider each reflection point.

FIGURE 1.2

Attunement Reflection: Identity

1	2	3	4	5	6	7	8	9	10
Rarely	During Times of Significant Transition		Annually			Quarterly		Monthly	Weekly/ Daily

Guiding Questions	Reflection
Look at the number line above. To what degree have you reflected on your own identity and the implications it has for your personal and professional growth? Why do you think this may be? What factors might encourage or discourage this reflection?	
How have *static* components of your identity (e.g., sex, race, ethnicity, national origin, first language) affected the way you project yourself externally?	
How have *dynamic* components of your identity become more salient or concrete over time? Such components include gender, nationality, socioeconomic status/income, sexual orientation, physical/emotional/developmental (dis)ability, age, religious or spiritual affiliation, education, occupation, work experience, organizational role, political ideology, and appearance.	
Which components of your identity feel flexible and fluid? Which components feel more rigid? Why do you think this is so?	
How has your identity development influenced you as a learner?	

Cultivate Your Capacity

Identify one component of your static or dynamic identity that defines who you are personally but does not tend to present itself in your professional life. Why do you think this is so? What actions might you (or your colleagues) take to enable you to show up more fully within your school community and experience greater harmony between your perceived and presented selves?

Cultivate Organizational Capacity

Are there ways you unintentionally make it difficult for others to present their full selves within your school community? Do they see and work with others who look and sound like them? Can individuals safely navigate the school building regardless of their abilities, age, or appearance? Is it safe to work there for all sexual orientations, religious or spiritual affiliations, and political ideologies? Where gaps exist, how will you be an ally and advocate to address them?

Drive

What gets you out of bed in the morning? What sparks your interest to try a new teaching or leading approach? What made you pick up this book? Motivation begins at a very young age and is a powerful force in the learning process, particularly for adults. We have come a long way from sticker charts and color-coded clip systems, and honestly, so has the research, but it is important to understand how motivational theory has evolved over time and shifts throughout our lifespan to fully grasp how it affects our drive for growth.

Hierarchy of Professional Needs

Many educators are familiar with Abraham Maslow's (1943) hierarchy of needs, a five-tier model that includes physiological needs, safety needs, love and belonging, esteem, and self-actualization. Maslow categorizes the first four levels of the model as "deficiency needs" and the final level (self-actualization) as a "growth need"; in other words, the deficiency needs must be met before we can experience growth. Whether we progress through an age-based model of personality development like Erikson's (1968) or a developmental one like Maslow's, learners' ability to move to the next level of growth is inhibited when the previous stage is not fully actualized. In this sense, educators who struggle to secure necessary resources or feel a sense of belonging in their school will most likely not experience self-efficacy in the classroom or seek to engage deeply in professional learning experiences. Their deficiency needs must be met first.

Schools typically apply Maslow's hierarchy of needs to students rather than educators, and as a result they view the tiers as being mostly grounded within the personal domain (e.g., how students' home experiences affect their academic growth and achievement). However, when considering these needs through an adult learning lens, it becomes equally important to ground the tiers within the professional domain.

Pause and Reflect

Pause to consider the hierarchy of needs in relation to your own professional experience. Figure 1.3 outlines the tiers of Maslow's model and provides guiding questions as well as reflection space for you to think about the degree to which your developmental needs are (or are not) currently being met.

FIGURE 1.3
Attunement Reflection: Hierarchy of Professional Needs

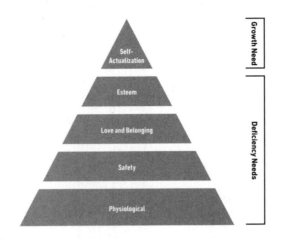

Tier	Guiding Questions	Reflection
Physiological	• Is there time during work hours for me to consume healthy food? • Do I have access to clean drinking water in my school? • Do my teaching and leading responsibilities allow for adequate rest?	
Safety	• Do the school building and climate feel safe to me? • Does my employment contract provide necessary protections? • Do I have the resources I need to feel secure and perform my job well?	
Love and Belonging	• Are there individuals I can turn to at work for both moral and professional support? • Is my school's culture inclusive? • Do I feel like I belong here? • Do I trust my colleagues?	
Esteem	• Am I confident in my professional abilities? • Do I have the capacity to meet students' and staff members' needs? • Do I feel a sense of achievement at work? • Do I respect others' work and do others respect mine?	
Self-Actualization	• Do I have creative autonomy to try new strategies and approaches in my work? • Do I have access to professional learning that is personalized and meets my individual needs? • Are my ideas welcomed and valued?	

When educators express concern about long hours and burnout, it typically signals that they are out of alignment (see Chapter 2) or that one or more of their professional needs is not being met. In fact, I often observe that individuals' concerns tend to center on one or two areas of focus (or tiers) throughout their careers, either because they get stuck there or because their school community does not fully cultivate their needs.

Cultivate Your Capacity

Review your reflection in Figure 1.3 and identify a tier where you may be stuck. Why do you think this is so? Do you need to seek out opportunities or experiences to provide you with a broader perspective? Do you feel limited by the constraints of your school's structure or standards of professional care? Note that it is possible to experience self-actualization and still not work in the place of best fit. However, focusing on specific areas of need can help you become better attuned to your sources of stress, better analyze and understand your feelings of exhaustion or exclusion, and become a stronger advocate for yourself and your colleagues. When experiences or concerns related to this professional area surface, consider journaling about them or making note of them in your planner so you are better equipped to understand them, recognize patterns, and grow through them.

Cultivate Organizational Capacity

Review your reflection in Figure 1.3 and identify a tier where your team, school, or district may be stuck or need improvement. What action steps might you recommend or actualize? What resources do you need? How and with whom will you advocate?

Expectancy and Value

As we work to build educator social-emotional capacity, we should pay special attention to the tiers of *esteem* and *self-actualization.* For far too long, the education field has taken a behaviorist or carrot-and-stick approach to adult professional growth. Prime examples of this include routinized teacher evaluation systems; emphasis on supervision over coaching; one-size-fits-all, "sit and get" professional development; and tracking clock hours rather than quality engagement and peer collaboration.

The degree to which we choose to engage in growth-oriented tasks is grounded in an expectancy-value model of achievement performance (Atkinson, 1957). Essentially, do we believe we will succeed or fail at a task (*expectancy*), and do we care (*value*)? Will the new instructional strategy we have been asked to try work in our classroom, and is it worth the time and effort to attempt with students? Can we implement a new teacher observation and coaching model, and would that be an effective use of our staffing and resources? Though much expectancy-value motivation research focuses mostly on upper-elementary students and adolescents (see, e.g., Eccles et al., 1983; Wigfield & Eccles, 1992), Bandura's (1977) related self-efficacy work examines adult learners.

Self-Efficacy

Like the expectancy-value model of motivation, self-efficacy theory looks beyond our sheer motivation to achieve a particular goal and examines the degree to which we believe the goal can be achieved—in essence, "I want ...," but also "I can ...." Self-efficacy, or our belief in ourselves, develops over time through four main sources of influence:

1. *Mastery experiences (performance outcomes):* "I did it before so I can do it again."
2. *Vicarious experiences (social role models):* "I have seen this teacher/ leader succeed with _____, so I probably can as well."
3. *Social persuasion:* "My colleague or leader believes I can be successful."
4. *Emotional and physiological states:* "I feel healthy and well, and I believe I can do this."

Our abilities are not fixed, and our belief in our abilities has a profound effect on our performance. As our self-efficacy strengthens, so does our capacity to bounce back from failure and approach challenges with a solution orientation (Bandura, 1997). Leaders can help their teams develop self-efficacy by emphasizing peer modeling, providing regular opportunities for feedback, encouraging participation and engagement as a learning community, and promoting self-accountability.

Autonomy and Personal Mastery

As we learn more about adult motivation, some elements continue to emerge as critically important to our developmental drive. Maslow's tier of self-actualization, which includes creative autonomy, is bolstered by Malcolm S. Knowles's principles of adult learning, which highlight adults' "deep need to be self-directing" (Knowles et al., 2005, p. 40). Unlike children or adolescents, who often look to a parent or teacher for guidance, adults seek a voice in their professional learning as well as opportunities for co-creation, social construction, and self-discovery (Rodman, 2019). In this way, growth of an organization is dependent upon the development of its learners, and in schools, this includes both students *and* adults. "Organizations learn only through individuals who learn," writes Senge (2006). "Individual learning does not guarantee organizational learning. But without it no organizational learning occurs" (p. 129).

Top-down learning misses the mark, inhibiting learners' autonomy and growth. Instead, we need to value educators' autonomy as well as their need for personal mastery. Personal mastery is just that—*personal*. Sometimes learners' individual visions and skills may align to the organization's goals, and sometimes there will be tension. Learners with high levels of personal mastery are continuously learning; they never "arrive."

Pause and Reflect
Pause to consider your own personal vision for growth (see Figure 1.4).

FIGURE 1.4

Attunement Reflection: Personal Vision for Growth

Guiding Questions	Reflection
In your ideal future, you are exactly the kind of person you want to be. What are your qualities?	
What material things do you own? Describe your ideal living environment.	
What have you achieved around health, fitness, athletics, and anything to do with your body?	
What types of relationships do you have with friends, family, romantic partners, and others?	
What is your ideal professional or vocational situation? If you are teaching, in what environment are you teaching; if not, what are you doing, and where? For teachers: What kind of teacher are you in your most desired future? How do your students see you? What impact do your efforts have?	
What are you creating for yourself in the arena of individual learning, travel, reading, or other activities?	
What kind of community or society do you live in?	
What else, in any other arena of your life, represents the fulfillment of your most-desired results?	
The discipline of personal mastery calls on us to make choices. What do we most want to do and become? And what do we perceive the world calling us to do and become? Choosing—picking the results and actions that you will make into your destiny—is a courageous act. When you consciously make a choice, you are more attuned, on every level, to the opportunities that come your way.	
I choose…	

Guiding questions from *Schools that learn: A fifth discipline fieldbook for educators, parents, and everyone who cares about education* (Senge, 2000, pp. 62, 63, 65).

Cultivate Your Capacity

Review your personal vision for growth from Figure 1.4. Focus on the impact of your efforts and what you are creating. Identify at least one specific step you can take in the next three months to move you closer toward this vision.

Cultivate Organizational Capacity

Incorporate your personal vision for growth into your work with your team. How do they envision their future work together, even if they're not in the same positions or school? What does their continued collaboration look like? How can they support one another in the next three months, six months, or year to move closer to their collective vision?

Growth Profile

Once we have established a strong sense of identity and an understanding of what drives us, we need to determine our ideal conditions for growth. If you could design the optimal environment for learning, what would it look, sound, and feel like? How would you orchestrate the dynamics among yourself, the leader or facilitator, and the other learners engaged in the experience? How would you co-create and socially construct new knowledge together? What would application and ongoing collaboration look like?

Educators recognize Howard Gardner's theory of multiple intelligences, and many consider these varied intellectual abilities in their lesson design and facilitation. We may have even self-diagnosed ourselves as individuals who are verbal-linguistic, logical-mathematical, visual-spatial, musical, naturalistic, bodily-kinesthetic, interpersonal, or intrapersonal (Gardner, 1983). Beyond our intellectual abilities, we can also consider our tendencies (that is, our responses to outer and inner expectations), types, and strengths as we build our own learner growth profile.

Following are some guideposts for educators who may not have considered other learning perspectives when reflecting on their own strengths and growth opportunities. When appropriate, links are provided to related assessments for you to explore (some free, some not) to support your developing understanding of yourself as a learner.

Tendencies: What We Expect and How We Respond

Children have expectations for school in the form of routines, procedures, communication dynamics, processing protocols, and so on. However, as learners mature, their reciprocal relationships with facilitators do as well. Professional learning facilitators expect as much, if not more, of their adult learners as adult learners do of them. Therefore, it is important for adult learners to understand their dominant tendency when responding to both outer expectations (e.g., meeting work deadlines, answering a request from a friend) and inner expectations (e.g., keeping a New Year's resolution, maintaining a yoga routine).

Gretchen Rubin (2018) has codified four tendencies that explain *why we act* and *why we do not act* as follows:

1. *Upholders* (19 percent) "respond readily to both outer expectations and inner expectations" (p. 6).
2. *Questioners* (24 percent) "question all expectations; they meet an expectation only if they believe it's justified, so in effect they respond only to inner expectations" (p. 6).
3. *Obligers* (41 percent) "respond readily to outer expectations but struggle to meet inner expectations" (p. 6).
4. *Rebels* (17 percent) "resist all expectations, outer and inner alike" (p. 6).

Rubin (2018) further notes that the "happiest, healthiest, most productive people aren't those from a particular Tendency, but rather they're the people who have figured out how to harness the strengths of their Tendency, counteract the weaknesses, and build the lives that work for them" (p. 12). As an educator, identifying your dominant tendency can help you better understand the expectations you have of students and colleagues as well as the ways in which you respond to their expectations of you.

Cultivate Your Capacity

Complete Gretchen Rubin's Four Tendencies Quiz (available for free at https://quiz.gretchenrubin.com) to identify your tendency and better understand how you respond to both outer and inner expectations. Then, use Figure 1.5 to outline how you will harness the strengths and counteract the weaknesses of your tendency.

FIGURE 1.5

Attunement Discipline in Practice: Tendencies

Identify the tendency with which you have the most alignment.

____ The Upholder ("Discipline is my freedom.")

____ The Questioner ("I'll comply—if you convince me why I should.")

____ The Obliger ("I'm counting on you to count on me.")

____ The Rebel ("You can't make me, and neither can I.") (Rubin, 2018)

How might you harness the strengths of your tendency?

How might you counteract the weaknesses of your tendency?

The Enneagram: Connecting the Dots

After one day in a classroom, an experienced educator can quickly identify the helpers, achievers, challengers, and peacemakers. The Enneagram is a typology of nine interconnected personality types. According to this model, individuals are born with a dominant personality type that does not change over time and typically has a "wing," or complementary personality type. While psychometric analysis of these personality types is limited, the Enneagram is regularly utilized in business contexts to guide workplace interpersonal dynamics, and it offers value in educational spaces as well, particularly with regard to intrapersonal attunement. The nine Enneagram types are as follows:

1. *The Reformer*—The rational, idealistic type: principled, purposeful, self-controlled, and perfectionistic
2. *The Helper*—The caring, interpersonal type: demonstrative, generous, people-pleasing, and possessive
3. *The Achiever*—The success-oriented, pragmatic type: adaptive, excelling, driven, and image-conscious
4. *The Individualist*—The sensitive, withdrawn type: expressive, dramatic, self-absorbed, and temperamental
5. *The Investigator*—The intense, cerebral type: perceptive, innovative, secretive, and isolated
6. *The Loyalist*—The committed, security-oriented type: engaging, responsible, anxious, and suspicious
7. *The Enthusiast*—The busy, fun-loving type: spontaneous, versatile, distractible, and scattered
8. *The Challenger*—The powerful, dominating type: self-confident, decisive, willful, and confrontational
9. *The Peacemaker*—The easygoing, self-effacing type: receptive, reassuring, agreeable, and complacent (The Enneagram Institute, n.d.)

Understanding both your own and others' Enneagram types can help you make connections among patterns of thinking and improve the quality of your communication, increasing self- and social awareness by highlighting the different filters through which we each make sense of the world. Enneagram types can also help us to find compatible thought and accountability partners, as those with the same type tend to be able to push each other further because they understand each other's motivations and patterns of thinking.

Cultivate Your Capacity

Complete the Riso-Hudson Enneagram Type Indicator (RHETI; available for $12.00 per test at www.enneagraminstitute.com/rheti). You can expect the test to take approximately 10 minutes to complete. While there are also free Enneagram tests, such as Truity (www.truity.com/test /enneagram-personality-test) and a variety of RHETI samplers, the paid RHETI test is the most popular, has been independently and scientifically validated, and produces a full personality profile across all nine Enneagram types. The Enneagram Institute also offers an Instinctual Variants Questionnaire (IVQ) to further define your understanding and support your understanding of others. Use Figure 1.6 to identify your dominant Enneagram type and wing as well as strong potential thought partners.

FIGURE 1.6

Attunement Discipline in Practice: Enneagram Types

Identify your dominant Enneagram type as well as your wing.

Dominant Type		Wing
1	The Reformer	——
2	The Helper	——
3	The Achiever	——
4	The Individualist	——
5	The Investigator	——
6	The Loyalist	——
7	The Enthusiast	——
8	The Challenger	——
9	The Peacemaker	——

Identify a thought partner with the same dominant type who might understand your motivations and patterns of thought.

Type Indicators: How We Act and What We Say

Full disclosure: My mother was a school psychologist, and I think I took my first Rorschach inkblot test at age 5. At the time, I barely knew clouds from clowns, but I have very vivid memories of completing my first Myers-Briggs Type Indicator (MBTI) test as a sophomore in high school. It (accurately?) pointed me toward education, and over time, only one metric of my profile has shifted—not in type, but rather manifestation. My maturity has taught me the value of listening (introversion) over speaking (extroversion). I exhibited extroversion quite freely at a younger age, but as I grow older, this facet of my personality has been replaced with a greater focus on quiet reflection and visioning. My dual professional role as both a coach and a speaker also requires that I manifest different shades of this function at various times, listening as a thought partner and projecting as a facilitator.

The MBTI is one of the oldest and most widely used profile tools. The original version, known as Form A, was copyrighted in 1943 and has been updated as recently as 2019 to global versions of the Step I and II assessments. It measures personality preferences (e.g., thinking or feeling) and helps individuals understand behavior and communication habits across 16 different personality types. The MBTI includes personality preferences in four key areas:

1. How you get your energy (extroversion versus introversion)
2. How you take in information and learn (sensing versus intuition)
3. How you make decisions (thinking versus feeling)
4. How you like to organize your time and environment (judging versus perceiving) (The Myers-Briggs Company, n.d.)

Katharine Cook Briggs and her daughter, Isabel Briggs Myers, originally designed the MBTI during World War II as a tool to help people better understand one another and minimize conflict. It continues to serve that purpose today, including through type indicator coaching and as a facilitation tool for teams.

The MBTI is a particularly critical tool for supporting educator wellness. Are you creating space in your schedule to recharge in the ways your personality requires? Are you engaging in professional learning that aligns to how you process and make sense of information? How are you organizing your time and space? In the daily grind of bell schedules and grading, it is easy to fall into the trap of reactively responding rather than proactively controlling our time and space (more on this in Chapter 2). The MBTI can help us harness our energy in ways that amplify our strengths.

Take myself, for example. Education conferences fuel my learning soul: I will hit the convention floor at 7:00 a.m., present a session, attend three more, and connect until all hours of the night with members of my professional learning network. These trusted colleagues kick back my half-baked ideas, field-test the solid ones, and share their own brilliance. However, what few people know is that my close introversion/extroversion split requires that I hide in my hotel room for a couple hours in the afternoon. Yes, this self-proclaimed professional learning geek and speaker skips some amazing conference sessions. Being attuned to my own personality type (and understanding that I need to recharge and rest) allows me to bring my best self to the experiences where I find the most value to accelerate my growth. Do not aim for balance; it is healthy to let go.

Cultivate Your Capacity

The Myers-Briggs Type Indicator (available for $49.95 at www.mbtionline.com or through a certified MBTI practitioner) takes approximately 45 minutes to complete. Following the test, utilize the learning paths in the MBTI online portal to support your area(s) for development.

A free MBTI-style assessment is the Open Extended Jungian Type Scale, or OEJTS (available online including at https://openpsychometrics.org/tests/OJTS). The OEJTS was developed as an open-source alternative to the MBTI, and a statistical analysis of the OEJTS and three other online MBTI alternatives found it to be the most accurate.

Use Figure 1.7 to make note of your MBTI personality type and identify how you will leverage it to source greater energy, process information more effectively and efficiently, make better decisions, and appropriately structure your action plans.

FIGURE 1.7
Attunement Discipline in Practice: Type Indicators

Select the appropriate value for your type indicator from each section below.

Energy Source
☐ E—Extrovert
☐ I—Introvert

Information Processing
☐ S—Sensor
☐ N—Intuitive

Decision-Making Approach
☐ T—Thinker
☐ F—Feeler

Structural Needs
☐ J—Judger
☐ P—Perceiver

How might you utilize your type indicator to source greater energy, process information more effectively and efficiently, make better decisions, and appropriately structure your action plans?

Strengths-Based Learning: Building from Your Core

Educators frequently examine problems of practice through a strengths-based rather than a deficit-based approach. We build on students' strengths to develop their skills rather than getting bogged down by their weaknesses. In the case of adult learners, however, most individuals overestimate their strengths: Four studies by Cornell University psychologists found that individuals who scored in the 12th percentile on tests of humor, grammar, and logic self-rated their expertise to be, on average, in the 62nd percentile (Kruger & Dunning, 1999). It is that much more important, then, for us to understand our true strengths rather than those we merely perceive if we are to build upon them and maximize our growth. "Recognizing my own limitations helps me to support young students as they face challenges and frustrations," shares Jennifer Orr, a National Board Certified elementary school teacher and author in Fairfax, Virginia. "Having been a classroom teacher for more than 20 years, I have worked with hundreds of students.... Knowledge of myself and honesty about that knowledge is crucial to my ethic of care as an educator, both with students and with colleagues."

The CliftonStrengths Assessment (formerly Clifton StrengthsFinder) was designed by educational psychologist Don Clifton. Like the MBTI, it was inspired by the World War II climate and a desire to do good for humankind. From 1949 to 1999, Clifton's work evolved through several iterations—first as a tool to help companies place employees in the positions that best fit their strengths and later to support individuals directly in identifying and maximizing their strengths. Educators may be familiar with the book *How Full Is Your Bucket?* that Don Clifton coauthored with his grandson Tom Rath and was published shortly after Clifton's death in 2003. The Clifton-Strengths Assessment continues to be updated, including with the latest release of the CliftonStrengths 34 Report (2018), which details individuals' competencies across 34 themes and the four domains of executing, influencing, relationship building, and strategic thinking (Gallup, 2022).

The CliftonStrengths approach evolved out of a simple question Clifton posed: "What would happen if we studied what was *right* with people versus what's wrong with people?" (Gallup, 2022). Much in the way a strengths-based approach works with students in the classroom, this tool provides a window into your own strengths and how you can best leverage them.

Cultivate Your Capacity

The CliftonStrengths Assessment ($19.99 to $59.99, available at www .gallup.com/cliftonstrengths) takes approximately 30 minutes to complete. The CliftonStrengths 34 assessment provides strategies to manage your potential weaknesses as well as strength-based resources. There are also

specific assessments for leaders as well as a CliftonStrengths Team Activities Guide available. CliftonStrengths offers student versions of its assessments along with volume-based rates if you wish to use the approach with
students in the classroom or across your staff.

Figure 1.8 provides you with space to capture your top five strengths as
well as outline how you plan to leverage these strengths in your work.

FIGURE 1.8
Attunement Discipline in Practice: Strengths-Based Learning

Identify your Top 5 CliftonStrengths from among the 34 strengths outlined in the four domains below.

Strategic Thinking
- Analytical
- Context
- Futuristic
- Ideation
- Input
- Intellection
- Learner
- Strategic

Influencing
- Activator
- Command
- Communication
- Competition
- Maximizer
- Self-Assurance
- Significance
- Woo

Relationship Building
- Adaptability
- Connectedness
- Developer
- Empathy
- Harmony
- Includer
- Individualization
- Positivity
- Relator

Executing
- Achiever
- Arranger
- Belief
- Consistency
- Deliberative
- Discipline
- Focus
- Responsibility
- Restorative

How do you plan to leverage these strengths in your work?

Character Strengths: Our Human Capacity

The Values in Action (VIA) Institute on Character, developed by Martin Seligman and Neal Mayerson, also takes a strengths-based approach, focusing on positive individual traits that are involved in the multiple dimensions of well-being. Led by Christopher Peterson and collaborating with a team of 55 other social scientists, Seligman and Mayerson identified six virtues (wisdom, courage, humanity, justice, temperance, and transcendence) and 24 character strengths or human capacities. They sought to find strengths that spanned both culture and time, were trait-like (i.e., manifested in a range of behaviors, thoughts, and feelings), and had cultural rituals for cultivating and sustaining them (among other criteria). These strengths are generally stable and do not change over time. It is also important to note that character strengths are shaped by context and do not operate in isolation from settings. In essence, our school cultures affect our individual strengths.

As we look to educators to model social-emotional learning for students, it is critical for us to understand strengths in our own executive functioning as well as our character. Social-emotional competency requires more than a series of lesson plans and community-building activities. Before we can work with students to develop their self-awareness, we have a responsibility to better know ourselves.

Cultivate Your Capacity

The VIA Character Strengths Survey (available for free at www
.viacharacter.org) takes approximately 15 minutes to complete. After taking the assessment, you will be provided with the opportunity to purchase a variety of different reports to guide your next steps. These include a Mindfulness and Character Strengths Report ($15.00), Top 5 Report ($19.00), and Total 24 Report ($49.00). Team reports are available as a $15 add-on feature for teams seeking to understand their members' unique strengths and how they work in combination. Youth reports are also available for students ages 10 to 17 ($10.00).

Use Figure 1.9 to capture your top five character strengths and outline how you plan to leverage the strengths in your work.

FIGURE 1.9
Attunement Discipline in Practice: Character Strengths

Identify your Top 5 character strengths from among the 24 strengths outlined in the six domains below.

Wisdom
- ☐ Creativity
- ☐ Curiosity
- ☐ Judgment
- ☐ Love of Learning
- ☐ Perspective

Courage
- ☐ Bravery
- ☐ Honesty
- ☐ Perseverance
- ☐ Zest

Humanity
- ☐ Kindness
- ☐ Love
- ☐ Social Intelligence

Justice
- ☐ Fairness
- ☐ Leadership
- ☐ Teamwork

Temperance
- ☐ Forgiveness
- ☐ Humility
- ☐ Prudence
- ☐ Self-Regulation

Transcendence
- ☐ Appreciation of Beauty and Excellence
- ☐ Gratitude
- ☐ Hope
- ☐ Humor
- ☐ Spirituality

How do you plan to leverage these strengths in your work?

Beyond identity and drive, understanding who we are as learners and how we respond to others is critical to our social-emotional growth. The capacity-building plan in Appendix A (p. 170) includes all the models and guideposts outlined in this section to help you identify which action steps you may want to consider next. Although one single guidepost will not provide you with a complete picture of who you are as a learner, collectively, these resources offer a window into your preferences and strengths and how you can best leverage them for continuous growth.

Cultivate Organizational Capacity

Of the growth profile models discussed in this chapter, which do you think might best meet your staff members' attunement needs? How might you facilitate a professional learning opportunity for them to collectively complete one of the assessments and then review and process the results and subsequent reports both individually and as a team? What might this continued work look like as it is revisited at multiple points throughout the school year? Are there opportunities to integrate these profiles and ongoing action steps into staff members' professional growth plans?

Attuning Our Perceived and Presented Selves

How we perceive ourselves manifests in how we present ourselves to others. Attunement occurs when our understanding and awareness of our inward selves harmonizes with the image we project to the external world. This comes naturally to some, whereas for others it requires much more tending. At times we feel the need to conceal or reveal personal information to influence others' perceptions (Human et al., 2012). Kelisa Wing, assessment branch chief for the Department of Defense Education Activity, a federal school system, shared the following with me:

> Understanding my own identity and how important those elements of my identity are allows me to be hypersensitive to the way others want to be identified. Identity development is so important—especially for people of color, who often see themselves through the lens of how the world views them. This truly does lead to cognitive dissonance—holding two competing thoughts within yourself. For this reason, identity is so important to me in understanding who we are, why we think the way we do, and what motivates and drives our actions.

Our social-emotional growth is rooted in the degree to which we can attune our identity, drive, and growth profile to the learning professional we present to others. Improving our attunement requires a commitment to consistent reflection—both inward and outward. Judy Brody, a former teacher and mentor and founder of the Aspiring Principals Program at the University of Pennsylvania's Graduate School of Education, told me the following:

> Improving practice became synonymous for me with becoming a reflective practitioner. This strategy continues to frame my learning with self and others. I frequently pose two deceptively simple questions: "Am I doing what I say I am doing?" [and] "What are the consequences of my behaviors?" I came to understand that the answers to those questions, as painful as they may be at times, would lead to authenticity for me in my practice, as well as [for] the adults I mentored.

Reflection helps us to harmonize who we are internally with how we present as learning professionals.

Although research is mixed on whether one-time or sustained professional learning has the greatest effect on *professional* growth, educators often feel more fulfilled from sustained experiences because they promote *social-emotional* growth. This may be why adult learners tend to gravitate toward affinity groups, book clubs, professional learning communities, mastermind groups, and team experiences rather than one-time workshops or conferences: We recognize that when trust builds over time, we are better able to attune our perceived and presented selves. Membership-based groups of the past are slowly being replaced by more informal networks, where the emphasis is on connection and relationships rather than access and titles.

As we seek to harmonize our perceived and presented selves, we should consider the qualities of our learning environments by reflecting on the following questions:

- Does this space operate as a true learning organization with a focus on personal mastery, mental models, shared vision, and team learning? Do the essences, principles, and practices of each of these disciplines align?
- Do the group norms, rituals, stories, and traditions of this organization's culture align with who I am and who I am working to become?

- Do I feel a sense of belonging in this space? Do I feel welcome here? Will I thrive?

Finding attunement is about knowing ourselves *and* seeking the spaces that will best cultivate our growth.

Attunement Integration Guide and Capacity-Building Plan

Given the reciprocal nature of our perceived and presented selves, it is helpful to develop the discipline of attunement through an attunement cycle. Attunement is an act of both perception (feeling to thinking) and processing (watching to doing). As outlined in Figure 1.10, concrete experiences (feeling) lead to reflection observations (watching). From there, we begin to form abstract conceptualizations (thinking), which transfer to active experimentation (doing). Then the cycle begins again as we feel, watch, think, and do.

FIGURE 1.10
Attunement Cycle

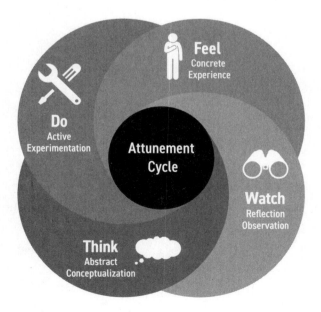

The stages of the cycle are based on David Kolb's (Kolb & Fry, 1974) experiential learning cycle.

According to Kolb and Fry (1974), the cycle in Figure 1.10 (the stages of which are based on their experiential learning cycle)

> provides a framework for the integration of cognitive and socio-emotional perspectives of the learning process. In the integration of these perspectives lies the possibility of a holistic approach to the learning process... [and of] the recognition and description of individual differences in learning styles. These styles shape behavior not only in traditional educational settings but shape an individual's basic mode of adaptation to the world about him. (p. 56)

In this way, consistent progression through the cycle helps us attune our perceived and presented selves.

Pause and Reflect

The integration guide in Appendix A (p. 169) brings these concepts together to guide your growth in the discipline of attunement as a learning professional. Pause here to review the integration guide and identify the next steps you will take to strengthen your capacity in this area.

The capacity-building plan in Appendix A (p. 170) captures all the action steps for your identity, drive, and growth profile outlined in this chapter.

Extend the Learning Loop

The resources outlined in Figure 1.11 may provide additional support as you continue developing the discipline of attunement. The list includes space for you to add your own resources for exploration as you develop a capacity-building plan for yourself and your team(s).

FIGURE 1.11

Recommended Resources: Attunement

☐ Harvard Graduate School of Education's EASEL Lab (https://easel.gse.harvard.edu)

☐ "A Theory of Human Motivation," in *Psychological Review,* by Abraham Maslow (1943)

☐ *Motivation and Personality* by Abraham Maslow (Harper & Row, 1954)

☐ *Self-Efficacy in Changing Societies* by Alfred Bandura, Editor (Cambridge University Press, 1997)

☐ *Self-Efficacy: The Exercise of Control* by Alfred Bandura (Worth, 1997)

☐ *Drive: The Surprising Truth About What Motivates Us* by Daniel Pink (Riverhead, 2011)

☐ *Frames of Mind: The Theory of Multiple Intelligences* by Howard Gardner (Basic Books, 2011)

☐ *The Four Tendencies: The Indispensable Personality Profiles That Reveal How to Make Your Life Better (and Other People's Lives Better, Too)* by Gretchen Rubin (Harmony, 2017)

☐ *Discovering Your Personality Type: The Essential Introduction to the Enneagram* by Don Richard Riso and Russ Hudson (HarperOne, 2003)

☐ *Introduction to Type® Series,* The Myers-Briggs Company (https://shop.themyersbriggs.com/en/mbtiproducts.aspx?pc=155)

☐ CliftonStrengths Books (https://store.gallup.com/c/en-us/5/books)

☐ VIA Character Strength Books (www.viacharacter.org/resources/books)

☐ *The Experiential Educator: Principles and Practices of Experiential Learning* by Alice Kolb and David Kolb (Experience Based Learning Systems, 2017)

☐

☐

☐

☐

Knowing ourselves and finding a synergistic relationship between our inner and outer beings—in other words, seeking attunement—is the first step in building adult social-emotional capacity, and this step requires deep commitment on the part of learners. Basil Marin, principal at Thomas Harrison Middle School in Virginia, shared the following with me:

> As a student, I was a "mismatch," a "misfit," a "pushout," and a "delinquent." By developing my self-awareness, owning my responsibility to develop myself, and committing to my education, I now hold a PhD and am a principal. I am the 2 percent—the paradigm shift you read about. Now I have a responsibility to model for my students that they have the potential to achieve the same. But that starts with a willingness and commitment to continue developing myself first.

As professionals deeply committed to our students, we must also have a strong commitment to ourselves. "If our goal is for children and youth to learn to be self-aware, to appreciate the perspective of others, to develop character and to demonstrate integrity, educators—both in and out of school—need to exemplify those behaviors within the learning community. When adults model these skills for young people, their own well-being improves," notes the Aspen Institute National Commission on Social, Emotional, and Academic Development (2019, p. 50). Students see our actions, they sense our authenticity, and quite honestly, they know when we are faking it. Educator capacity building begins with a commitment to your own attunement.

2

ALIGNMENT

> When in doubt, check if your actions
> are aligned with your purpose.
>
> —Azim Jamal and Brian Tracy

Out of Alignment

align (verb): to arrange in a straight line; to adjust according to a line

Regardless of school type, class size, student population, or learning culture, a universal challenge for educators is the need for more time. The days never seem to have enough hours; the evenings and weekends never feel fully your own. While personal and professional boundaries blur across professions, they appear particularly blended in education. Despite this, other fields perceive educators as having afternoons and summers "off" with no professional or administrative responsibilities beyond the final bell. Educator burnout is real: An estimated 44 percent of teachers in public and private schools leave teaching within five years of entry (Ingersoll et al., 2018). At the same time, the American Association of Colleges for Teacher Education (2022) reports that undergraduate enrollment in undergraduate teaching programs continues to decline. Educators are, in a word, *tired,* and the pauses they do have consist of quick bursts to reset or recharge rather than truly recover. Collectively, we need to establish more sustainable systems and approaches that keep educators in the game and fully present for themselves and their students. We can certainly better leverage time, space, and connection at the systems level (see Rodman et al., 2020), but here we will focus on the self—how you, as an individual, can create stronger alignment between your purpose and practice.

Given the complexity of educators' responsibilities, many tend to be extreme organizers. Their planners and calendars are color-coded works of art. Their classrooms (both physical and virtual) corral thousands of resources and file them in precise locations for retrieval. Lists and labels make routines and procedures hum like a well-orchestrated symphony. Educators do not lack time because they are disorganized, but because their purpose (i.e., the goals they set for themselves and their students) and their practice (i.e., how they spend their time) are out of sync.

For adult learners, then, self-management is less about "finding" time than about alignment. The discipline of alignment calls on us to create congruence between our purpose and our practice. Everyone possesses the same 168 hours per week; it is how we choose to utilize them that makes the difference between goal setting and goal attainment, between operating in survival mode and the recovery zone, and between burnout and fulfillment. Educators do not have a *time* deficit but, rather, an *alignment* one. Figure 2.1 provides an alignment blueprint to guide your exploration of this discipline.

> As you read this chapter, you can use the QR code or visit https://www .thelearningloop.com/book-alignment to access editable PDF versions of the reflection and planning tools included throughout the text. Use the case-sensitive password "StillLearning" to download the resources.

FIGURE 2.1

Capacity-Building Blueprint: Alignment

Congruence Between Purpose and Practice		
Purpose	**=**	**Practice**
Goals Who we aim to be	**Self-Direction**	**Structured Time** chronotypes, time blocks, and tuning techniques
		Disciplined Action habits, stacking, and sticking
		Cadence of Accountability partners, playbooks, and pauses

Establishing Purpose

Ask educators what prompted them to enter the profession, and many will respond that they were inspired by a meaningful interaction with one of their own teachers or a desire to make an impact. But because it is a passion-driven profession, once educators enter the field, they can find it hard to define what success looks like—or, put another way, to articulate their purpose as teachers and leaders.

Defining Success

We know that effective educators produce more than students who demonstrate consistent reading growth, mathematical problem-solving skills, strong test scores, and high graduation rates (though these are certainly accomplishments to celebrate). We also know that these results are often confounded by other variables that do not diminish, but rather amplify, educators' work (e.g., students' [dis]abilities, students' socioeconomic status, school resources). As noted in the Introduction, educating the whole child requires tending to the tenets of health, safety, engagement, support, and challenge. It also requires supporting students' social-emotional learning, including self-awareness, self-management, social awareness, relationship skills, and responsible decision making. However, these metrics cannot be measured in the same way we might examine business growth, sales, or market shares. Educators need to establish purpose through a growth-oriented lens rather than a results-focused one. We need to ask, "What do we want to achieve?" but also "Who do we want to become?"

In a people-building field, widget-driven models are insufficient. This work is personal, not prescriptive.

Pause and Reflect

Revisit your personal vision for growth from Chapter 1 (Figure 1.4, p. 28) and ask, "Who do I want to become—for myself, my partner/family, my students, and my profession?"

Bucket Lists and Gold Stars

One of the most effective ways to establish purpose is to make a bucket list. Although this may seem contrived, visioning exercises help us clarify who we want to become both personally and professionally. Vision boards, annual and quarterly goals, and regular retreats (even solo ones) provide clarity on our progress toward our personal vision for growth.

Reach far and dream big here. Does success look like all your students finishing the year reading above grade level? Do you want 100 percent of your students to graduate on time with clear postsecondary plans? Perhaps you want to visit a particular country, run a marathon, or read at least 50 books this year. Push yourself to draft a bucket list with more than 20 items. Dig into your passions and pursuits beyond the point of comfort to quantify and clearly describe what constitutes achievement for you.

As educators, we provide students with multiple achievement metrics and co-develop goals with them by academic year and quarter. We track their growth with some form of "gold stars," whether via a benchmark assessment, class grade, or actual sticker sheet. We do this because progress matters. Recall that motivation is a confluence of both value ("I want...")

and expectancy ("I can..."). Yet somehow, as we get older, the gold stars fade even though the importance of self-efficacy does not. We feel as though we are losing time because we do not always have a clear vision of exactly what we are aiming toward.

Pause and Reflect

Pause here and use Figure 2.2 to draft your bucket list. Add one item per day for the next month if that feels more manageable and use your personal vision for growth from Chapter 1 for inspiration. You might also consider "life accounts" in your circle of being (spiritual, intellectual, physical, emotional), circle of relating (marital, parental, social), and circle of doing (vocational, avocational, financial) to guide your reflection (Hyatt & Harkavy, 2016). Your goals need not be distributed proportionately, particularly if some require more intensive development than others, but this tool will help you consider all areas of your personal vision. Do not limit your bucket list to educational and professional pursuits, either: Reflect on relationships, health, education, finance, creativity, entertainment, adventure, and travel as you brainstorm. You are also encouraged to add to and refine this list over time as you further clarify your ideal future.

Cultivate Your Capacity

Post your bucket list somewhere you will see it regularly. Revisit the list monthly to assess your progress toward one or more of your goals, and return to the list quarterly to set more goals and prioritize actions.

FIGURE 2.2

Alignment Reflection: Goals Bucket List

Life Accounts		Goals
Circle of Being	• **Spiritual** (Ex.: Visit a place of spiritual significance.) • **Intellectual** (Ex.: Earn a PhD.) • **Physical** (Ex.: Run a marathon in every state.) • **Emotional** (Ex.: Develop a regular meditation practice.)	1. 2. 3. 4. 5. 6. 7. 8.
Circle of Relating	• **Marital** (Ex.: Take an annual vacation with partner or spouse.) • **Parental** (Ex.: Plan a quarterly special event with each child.) • **Social** (Ex.: Go stargazing with a group of friends.)	9. 10. 11. 12. 13. 14.
Circle of Doing	• **Vocational** (Ex.: Become a mentor or present at a conference.) • **Avocational** (Ex.: Grow a garden or take a dance class.) • **Financial** (Ex.: Pay off debt or start a savings plan.)	15. 16. 17. 18. 19. 20.

Cultivate Organizational Capacity

Facilitate conversations with team members about items on their bucket lists. What education and skills do they want to refine or grow? Where do they want to travel, or what adventures do they want to experience? Can you support one another's bucket list goals related to creative pursuits or community contributions?

The Power of Three

As it turns out, things really do happen in threes. McKinsey and Company, among others, recommend that *three* is the optimal number of goals to tackle simultaneously (Christensen et al., 2021). When we take on more than that, the path gets muddy. We lose focus, feel overwhelmed, and revert to old patterns of practice. It becomes challenging to establish consistent and sustainable habits that drive us toward our goals. Aim for less, and you may be selling yourself short.

Review your bucket list and identify three goals you can reasonably accomplish within the next calendar year. Commit to them, *choose* them, go ahead and star them (yes, with gold stars if you have them handy). If a goal feels particularly weighty, chunk it into smaller segments. Identify which specific targets you will tackle in the next quarter. The intent here is clear purpose and progress. You want to be consistently aiming toward your personal vision for growth. When possible, select one goal from each of your circles of being, relating, and doing. This will enable you to feel whole personally, connect with others, and experience professional progress. It will also promote feelings of recovery, belonging, and fulfillment rather than burnout.

Goal Setting

You tell your students they are smart almost every day. You have probably even drafted SMART goals (those that are specific, measurable, achievable, relevant, and time-bound) for them with elements such as "student growth objectives." When it comes to crafting your own growth goals, consider Michael Hyatt's model of SMARTER goals—specific, measurable, actionable, risky, time-keyed, exciting, and relevant—instead:

- **Specific:** Detail exactly what you want to accomplish.
- **Measurable:** Try to quantify (not just qualify) the result.
- **Actionable:** Start with an active verb rather than a passive one (e.g., *quit, run, finish, eliminate*)
- **Risky:** Go right up to the edge of your comfort zone, then step over it.
- **Time-keyed:** Plan a date for delivery; end every goal with a deadline.
- **Exciting:** Choose goals that motivate you.
- **Relevant:** Ensure that your goals coordinate with your values, season in life, and other goals. (Hyatt, 2020)

Do not limit yourself; expand the notion of what is possible. Do you want to teach in Italy and live in government-funded housing on the Amalfi Coast? I have collaborated with educators who have done this and so much more. At times, my riskiest moves as an educator have left me flat on my face with embarrassment. Other times, I've gained opportunities I never would have experienced otherwise. I have had the opportunity to collaborate with paradigm-shifting innovators, visit amazing places, and engage in dinner conversations with my own education heroes because I was not afraid to take risks. I have also missed deadlines because of my (over)commitment to getting it right. In all cases, I learned and grew.

Risky goals must excite you; otherwise, you will find them terrifying rather than exhilarating. According to Locke and Latham (2013), "There is a linear relationship between the degree of goal difficulty and performance." In a review of almost 400 studies, they concluded that "the performance of participants with the highest goals was over 250% higher than those with the easiest goals" (p. 5). When we set challenging goals, we rise to meet them; when we take it easy, we sit back.

Pause and Reflect

Figure 2.3 provides you with space to sketch out your three SMARTER goals along with examples and nonexamples to guide you. Notice that the examples are not all time-keyed for end-of-year completion (e.g., June 30 for school-related goals or December 31 for calendar-related ones). We tend to put off goals that seem far away, and then they stack up beyond our ability to complete them. When drafting your goals, consider how they might be segmented by day, week, month, or quarter as well as year to optimize your growth. Also, recognize that some goals are achievement-oriented whereas others are more habit-driven. For habit-driven goals, where possible, include the location where you plan to meet the goal to make it "stickier" (e.g., walk in the park). (We will dig into this concept of place more deeply later in this chapter.)

FIGURE 2.3

Alignment Reflection: SMARTER Goals

Circle of Being	
Nonexamples and Examples	*Intellectual* ✗ Make more time for reading. ✓ Read one print book and listen to one audiobook per month. *Physical* ✗ Be more health conscious. ✓ Walk for 30 minutes at the park every weekday at 6:00 a.m.
Goal 1 ☐ Spiritual ☐ Intellectual ☐ Physical ☐ Emotional	SMARTER Goal:
Circle of Relating	
Nonexamples and Examples	*Social* ✗ Get to know my colleagues outside work. ✓ Have coffee with a new colleague at least one Friday per month. *Parental* ✗ Spend more time with my children. ✓ Schedule and plan a one-on-one day with each child per quarter.
Goal 2 ☐ Marital ☐ Parental ☐ Social	SMARTER Goal:
Circle of Doing	
Nonexamples and Examples	*Vocational* ✗ Develop my students' love of reading. ✓ Collaborate with community partners to add 100 new student-selected books to my classroom library by December 15. ✗ Improve teachers' instructional practice. ✓ Review teacher needs assessment and observation data and student achievement and growth data to select six key areas of focus for professional learning community implementation by November 1.
Goal 3 ☐ Vocational ☐ Avocational ☐ Financial	SMARTER Goal:

Cultivate Your Capacity

Include the three goals you drafted in Figure 2.3 in your planner. Revisit them weekly and integrate them into your daily planning and prioritization.

Cultivate Organizational Capacity

In weekly or monthly meetings with your team members, inquire about their progress on their SMARTER goals. Incorporate a regular cadence of accountability for one another (more on this later in the chapter).

Goals do not need to be *achievable* in the short term, but they do need to be *actionable* so you can work toward them. If not, they represent pipe dreams and possibilities, not a clear purpose for action you can weave into your daily routine. What if all your teachers became National Board Certified and your school was recognized as a teaching lab for innovative instructional practice? What if all your students constructed an action plan for addressing your community's biggest challenge and presented it to the mayor and city council with clear next steps bolstered by community support? What if we envisioned schools as incubators for positive and sustainable change rather than simply as portals for child care and development? What if we dared to be amazing and surmount the status quo? How would we structure our time to make it all happen? It's time to move from vision to action.

Structured Time

In our goal-setting processes, we tend to focus a lot more on the *why* and the *what* of our targets than on the *when*. We crowd more tasks into fewer blocks and wonder why we are not making progress. To align our purpose and practice requires paying attention to the timing of our actions as much as to the reasons for them. *When* we start on an action—be it a goal, habit, or task—has a lot to do with whether we complete it or integrate it consistently into practice.

The Importance of Timing and Fresh Starts

There is a reason so many of us set New Year's resolutions. Our brains establish temporal landmarks to help us construct stronger beginnings. In the same way we set spatial landmarks (e.g., "turn right at the field"), our brains are wired for new beginnings grounded in social landmarks (e.g., the first of the month, Mondays, national holidays) and personal landmarks (e.g., birthdays, anniversaries, religious holidays, new semesters, job changes). Both of these kinds of temporal or time-based landmarks allow us to interrupt our day-to-day actions, break with the past, and set a refined vision for our future selves. Leveraging temporal landmarks with time-keyed goals can help us maximize these fresh starts.

Consider how you might utilize temporal landmarks such as the start of a new school year, academic quarter, unit, or topic both for yourself and with your students. Do these fresh starts provide more opportunities for you and your students to integrate new strategies and skills, develop stronger habits, and maximize your growth?

Although midpoints and endings also hold power for goal acceleration and accomplishment, for many educators, the "starting" and "sticking" pose the greatest challenge; questions such as "Where do I start?" and "How do I fit this in?" emerge more often than "How do I push this to completion?"

Pause and Reflect

Pause here to identify at least three social or personal temporal landmarks that you might utilize as launchpads for goal attainment.

Temporal Landmarks

1. _____   ☐ Social   ☐ Personal
2. _____   ☐ Social   ☐ Personal
3. _____   ☐ Social   ☐ Personal

Cultivate Your Capacity

Make a note of the temporal landmarks you identified within your calendar or planner either on the exact day or one month prior. If possible, match these temporal landmarks to one of the bucket list items in Figure 2.2 (p. 52) or SMARTER goals in Figure 2.3 (p. 55). This will support you with stronger implementation and, in turn, more consistent goal attainment as you plan out each quarter.

Cultivate Organizational Capacity

Consider how you might leverage an institutional or site-based shared calendar to capture and highlight possible temporal landmarks for your learning community. While we frequently think of the beginning of academic quarters as "fresh starts" (and they certainly are), we might also draw on mid-quarter dates, community rituals or events, and significant transition points to establish temporal landmarks for learners across our system.

Chronotypes: Leveraging Peak Performance Time

Chronotypes such as morning larks and night owls are not folklore but, rather, a key component to maximizing our potential. Because school days are heavily structured, educators often dismiss this opportunity for stronger purpose and practice alignment, conforming instead to the established patterns of bells, buses, and prep periods. However, understanding and leveraging your chronotype can enhance overall performance. Formally, chronotypes are the behavioral manifestations of the circadian rhythms we experience throughout the day and night; informally, they are our internal body clocks.

The concept of chronobiology emerged at the turn of the 20th century, when German psychiatrist Emil Kraepelin noticed that some of his patients preferred to wake up and go to bed early while others were more productive in the evening hours (Becker et al., 2016). Kraepelin and his students later conducted a series of sleep studies that affirmed the existence of morning larks and night owls. This work was expanded in 1976 with the first chronotype assessment, and then again years later with the Munich Chronotype Questionnaire (MCTQ), which examined people's patterns on workdays versus free days (Roenneberg et al., 2003).

More recent chronobiology research has extended these types even further (Dockrill, 2020). "Afternooners" feel sleepy in the morning and evening and hit peak performance somewhere between 11:00 a.m. and 3:00 p.m. "Nappers" prefer to use this afternoon block for rest and kick into high gear on either side of this respite (Putilov et al., 2019). The most recent research shows a total of six human chronotypes, as outlined in Figure 2.4. A survey of 2,283 participants found that 95 percent self-assessed as one of the following six chronotypes: morning type or lark (13 percent), evening type or owl (24 percent), daytime sleepy type or napper (18 percent), daytime type or afternooner (15 percent), highly active type (9 percent), and moderately active type (16 percent) (Putilov et al., 2021).

FIGURE 2.4

Six Patterns of Diurnal Variation or Chronotypes

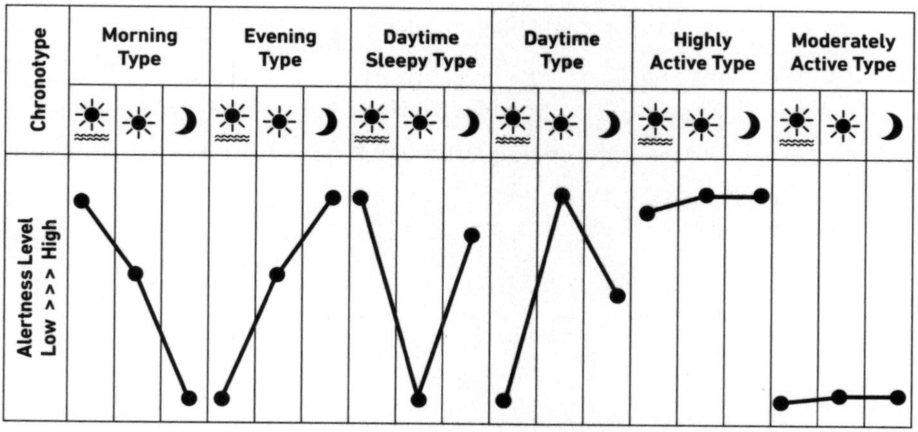

It is worth noting that the participants included in this most recent study were university students with a mean age of 22.1 years. Unlike the personality types examined in Chapter 1, which typically remain static throughout an individual's life, chronotypes can be affected by a person's age as well as gender, genetics, and even the time of year we're born.

Understanding your chronotype can help you structure your days in a way that maximizes productivity and goal achievement. For example, if instructional planning requires a heavier cognitive lift than grading or parent communication and you are a daytime type, it may benefit you to allocate morning or evening time for reviewing student assignments and an afternoon prep period for planning. Similarly, principals who are morning types may benefit from observing classrooms during first or second period and holding parent or administrative meetings later in the day. An understanding of chronotypes can be useful outside your professional life as well. Our chronotypes can suggest the best times for us to engage in high-output activities such as workouts versus lower-output ones like running errands or online shopping.

Aligning purpose and practice goes beyond creating a list of goals and crafting an action plan. We can better leverage time to make it happen.

Pause and Reflect

Return to Figure 2.4 and identify the chronotype that best matches your alertness level and energy flow at different times of the day. Then, note your chronotype in Figure 2.5 and consider how you might leverage it in your daily routines to accelerate growth. How might you purpose each core time block of a typical day?

FIGURE 2.5

Alignment Reflection: Chronotypes

After identifying your chronotype, consider how it might guide you as you purpose each core time block of a typical day.

Chronotype		Time
☐	Morning Type	5:00 a.m.
☐	Evening Type	6:00 a.m.
☐	Daytime Sleepy Type	7:00 a.m.
☐	Daytime Type	8:00 a.m.
☐	Highly Active Type	9:00 a.m.
☐	Moderately Active Type	10:00 a.m.

	11:00 a.m.
	12:00 p.m.
	1:00 p.m.
	2:00 p.m.
	3:00 p.m.
	4:00 p.m.
	5:00 p.m.
	6:00 p.m.
	7:00 p.m.
	8:00 p.m.
	9:00 p.m.
	10:00 p.m.

Cultivate Your Capacity

If you do not know or are unsure about your chronotype, there are a variety of auto-scored and self-scored tools you can use to focus on the time of day when you thrive the most. Here are some resources to get you started:

- Automated Morningness-Eveningness Questionnaire (Auto-MEQ): www.chronotype-self-test.info
- MCTQ Core: https://thewep.org/documentations/mctq/item /english-mctq-core
- MCTQ Full: https://thewep.org/documentations/mctq/item /english-mctq-full
- MCTQ for Children and Adolescents: https://thewep.org /documentations/mctq/item/english-mctq-full-children

Cultivate Organizational Capacity

Facilitate conversations with team members about their chronotypes and reflect on ways you may be able to support one another's efficiency and effectiveness. For example, an evening type who collaborates with a team of mostly morning types may prefer to respond to emails late in the evening but schedule them to send the next morning. Daytime sleepy type team members may find it hard to pay attention during afternoon meetings and prefer to connect at another time. To the extent it is possible, sync up meeting and planning times so most members can contribute at optimal performance levels.

Time Blocking: You Have More Time Than You Think

Bell schedules and prep periods drive the behavior patterns of most schools. We move from class to class, prep to lunch, meeting to home. As compared with other fields, daily schedules in education are quite monotonous. Because of this, educators tend to conceptualize their time as days with 24 hours to fill instead of as a week with 168 hours to structure and maximize. A deeper understanding of the week allows us to apportion our time more effectively for stronger results.

Laura Vanderkam (2011) has studied thousands of time logs, from both everyday people and some of the most successful individuals in the world, and she has found a "fundamental flaw in the data used to support the claim that we suffer from time poverty and overwork: we lie" (p. 19). When we compare survey data with actual time logs, we overestimate how much time we spend working, housecleaning, and caring for children. In fact, the more people claim they work, the more inaccurate these claims tend to be. For example, individuals who claimed to work 75 hours per week generally logged about 55. In reality, both males and females work less, clean less, and play with our children less than we did decades ago. Reciprocally, we underestimate our leisure time. We claim to have less than 16.5 hours of leisure time available per week after work and household responsibilities, yet simultaneously report watching more than 16.5 hours of television within the same 168-hour period. The challenge is not the hours available, but our preoccupation with busyness and multitasking.

Over time, our society has come to (over)value a commitment to work that is measured by clock hours over quality actions. We take note of who pulls into the parking lot first and leaves last. We know which staff members rush out immediately after the final bell and which are still planning and grading hours later. While I am not proposing we lock every school building by 4:00 p.m., there are healthier practices we can model and support to reduce educator burnout and more intentionally focus our work hours. The most effective and successful workers across professions log 35 to 40 extremely focused and targeted hours of work per week, and they approach their household, family, and leisure time with the same level of precision.

Our perception of time is clouded by how we classify and manage it. For example, as both a teacher and an administrator, I was guilty of responding to work emails late in the evening while watching television. I would have classified this as "work" rather than "leisure" time, but these hours were completely unfocused. A more effective (and sustainable) use of my time would have been spending 15 to 30 minutes responding to the most urgent requests, closing my laptop, and then fully enjoying this leisure time at the end of the day. Instead, I remained plugged in—and over time, I burned out. Similarly, at school I did not always guard my prep periods with intention and focus. I multitasked between copying, grading, planning, connecting with colleagues, and returning parent phone calls and emails rather than optimizing each part of my day to align with my chronotype and personal and professional goals. I felt "busy," so it seemed as though I was accomplishing a fair amount and making progress—until I reviewed my action plan and saw how much was still left to tackle. "On a neurological basis, the human brain does not really process multiple tasks at once," writes Vanderkam (2011). "Instead, it toggles back and forth, losing time on every switch. The more complex the tasks, the more time lost....Multitasking is, more often than not, inefficient single-tasking" (p. 196).

To single-task effectively, we need to classify our task types and, subsequently, the time blocks with which we structure our day. Charlie Gilkey, author of *Start Finishing: How to Go from Idea to Done* (2019), identifies four major time blocks that constitute most professionals' days: focus blocks, social blocks, administrative blocks, and recovery blocks. As an educator, I would also add student connection blocks to this list. For teachers, these consist of actual class time—not additional help before or after school, parent contact, or responding to student emails. For administrators, these include student arrival and dismissal and, when necessary, lunch supervision. I intentionally refer to this time block as student connection rather than student contact (as it is often referred to in contract terms) because it reframes how we can potentially purpose both instructional and administrative time for relationship building and, subsequently, shift this component of our professional responsibilities away from other available time blocks. Figure 2.6 provides an outline of time blocks, their typical length, and teacher and administrator tasks they might encompass.

Gilkey's work as well as other time-related research shows that hours spent with one's partner or family are typically categorized as recovery blocks. However, I find that we tend to multitask during these blocks more than any of the others. As a result, what was planned as recovery time becomes multipurposed as time to play with children, complete chores, return a phone call to a friend, and squeeze in a workout. Chores belong in an administrative block, and the phone call in a social block. In this convoluted jumble, it may only be the workout that brings us true recovery. If this resonates with you, it may be valuable to add a personal connection block to your stack so time with those in your circle of relating does not become muddled with dishes and laundry and your true recovery time is preserved as such. However, the goal here is simplicity: Do not overly complicate your calendar with more than the time blocks outlined.

FIGURE 2.6

School-Based Time Blocks and Task Types

Time Block	Teacher Tasks	Administrator Tasks
Focus Blocks *90–120 Minutes* Blocks of time when we are especially creative, inspired, and able to do high-level work that requires focus	• Instructional planning • Student/peer feedback • Grading • Professional learning	• Strategic planning • Observation feedback • Professional learning
Social Blocks *90–120 Minutes* Blocks of time when we are primed and energetically in the right space to meet other people	• Student support • Team meetings • Parent contact/meetings	• Leadership/board meetings • Team meetings • Parent contact/meetings
Administrative Blocks *30–60 Minutes* Lower-energy blocks of time when we are not in the zone to do the work that requires heavy lifting but there are still other types of work we can do effectively	• Email • Recordkeeping • Photocopying • Filing	• Email • Reporting • Budgeting/invoicing • Reviews and approvals
Student Connection Blocks *Variable Length*	• Class time	• Student arrival/dismissal • Lunch supervision • Classroom observations
Recovery Blocks *Variable Length* Blocks of time that we use for activities that recharge us, such as exercise, meditation, self-care, and intentional idling	• Walk with a colleague • Midday meditation	• Walk with a colleague • Midday meditation

Professional learning facilitator, teacher coach, and coauthor of *The Minimalist Teacher* Tammy Musiowsky-Borneman reiterated to me the importance of simplicity:

> My love for structures, systems, and planners stems from a lifetime of loving those things about school. So it made sense that when I started my work in education, I not only kept learning about structures and routines, I had a classroom and professional space to test and refine systems over time. In recent years, I have come to value flexibility, simplicity, and efficiency in my self-management systems the most. When planning out my day, generally I will section it into short chunks of work time that are often categorized as catch-up, consumption, and creation.

I recognize most teachers' schedules will not allow for 90- to 120-minute social blocks within their bell schedule, but we can still be thoughtful about how we stack each of these components within each week. A typical 40-hour teacher workweek might break down as follows:

- Student connection (class time): 25 hours
- Focus (instructional planning, feedback, grading, professional learning): 7.5 hours
- Social (student support, team meetings, parent contact/meetings): 2.5 hours
- Administrative (email, recordkeeping, photocopying, filing): 2.5 hours
- Recovery (walk with a colleague, midday meditation): 2.5 hours

The Organisation for Economic Co-operation and Development (OECD) found that public school primary teachers teach an average of 784 hours per year, lower-secondary teachers teach 711 hours, and upper-secondary teachers teach 684 hours (OECD, 2022). While the number of teaching hours in the United States is above the OECD average at all grade levels, it has remained mostly static from 2000 to 2005 to 2012—though the last decade has seen an increase in teaching hours among secondary teachers.

The Programme for International Student Assessment (PISA) is a triennial survey of 15-year-old students around the world that assesses the extent to which they have acquired the key knowledge and skills essential for full participation in society. The assessment focuses on the core school subjects of reading, mathematics, and science, with an optional financial literacy section. It is interesting to note that 2018 PISA results demonstrate U.S. students scoring above the OECD average in reading (505 compared with 487) and science (502 compared with 489), and below average in mathematics (478 compared with 489). This is not a new trend, but instead has been stable or increased in reading since 2000, science since 2006, and mathematics since 2003. On all three measures, U.S. students received similar or lower scores to students in Australia, Japan, New Zealand, Sweden, and the United Kingdom, yet students in these countries attend school for fewer instructional minutes (National Center for Education Statistics, 2020; Schleicher, 2019). It is not the hours, then, but how we purpose them that matters—for both students and educators.

When sketching out your model week, time allocations won't necessarily equate to 1.5 hours of focus time per day. Perhaps you notice that you engage in your strongest and most focused planning on Mondays and Tuesdays but grow tired by the end of the week; if so, concentrate your focus time blocks on Mondays and Tuesdays as much as possible. Maybe you prefer to grade and provide student feedback in the school building so you don't need to transport papers and projects to and from school (yet another transition). Use your prep period for grading rather than planning.

When crafting a model week, input your student connection time first. This is immovable as part of a master schedule and your top priority. Next, add consistently scheduled team meetings (e.g., department/curriculum, grade level, leadership). If these meetings average out to more than 90 minutes per week, your team may need to revisit its communication norms and agenda setting. Are you weighing down collaboration time with straightforward communication (better positioned in an email), or is this time being purposed for team connection and consultation?

Now, revisit your chronotype. When do you have the greatest energy for focus tasks versus social ones? Ideally, you would schedule two flexible 30-minute social blocks for parent contact or meetings and apportion the remaining time for focus tasks. Try to be as intentional as possible in your planning. Perhaps you designate five or six hours across Monday, Tuesday, and Wednesday for instructional planning and provide the bulk of your student feedback and grading in the latter part of the week. If feedback is consistent and timely, you can provide it verbally each day in class and in writing weekly. In your time blocking, however, be mindful of not grading for completion, which sends the message that the work is an act of student compliance, not content/skill mastery, and is a misuse of both of your time. Feedback, even more so than the grades, is critical in the learning process.

Speaker, author, and chief illuminator of Ignite Your S.H.I.N.E. LaVonna Roth shared with me how she uses time blocks to structure her work: "I block off all of my days. In the morning, my time is focused on creation, and in the afternoon, the focus is on connection. I am most creative in the morning so anything that requires big picture thinking, design, and strategy gets scheduled there. Then I do my best to schedule phone calls and webinars and respond to emails in the afternoon." Days should be driven by goals rather than task lists. Leveraging our chronotype while intentionally time blocking helps us align purpose to practice.

Pause and Reflect

Pause here to identify the time blocks you will use to structure your time:

Time Block	Length (in minutes)	Frequency (number per week)
1. _____	_____	_____
2. _____	_____	_____
3. _____	_____	_____
4. _____	_____	_____
5. _____	_____	_____
6. _____	_____	_____

Position these time blocks into the model week blueprint in Figure 2.7.

FIGURE 2.7

Alignment Discipline in Practice: Model Week Blueprint

Weekday	
Time	*Activity*
6:00 a.m.	
7:00 a.m.	
8:00 a.m.	
9:00 a.m.	
10:00 a.m.	
11:00 a.m.	
12:00 p.m.	
1:00 p.m.	
2:00 p.m.	
3:00 p.m.	
4:00 p.m.	
5:00 p.m.	
6:00 p.m.	
7:00 p.m.	
8:00 p.m.	
9:00 p.m.	

Weekend	
Time	*Activity*
6:00 a.m.	
7:00 a.m.	
8:00 a.m.	
9:00 a.m.	
10:00 a.m.	
11:00 a.m.	
12:00 p.m.	
1:00 p.m.	
2:00 p.m.	
3:00 p.m.	
4:00 p.m.	
5:00 p.m.	
6:00 p.m.	
7:00 p.m.	
8:00 p.m.	
9:00 p.m.	

Use this template to craft your ideal week and help you begin setting boundaries around different task types to maximize your efficiency and effectiveness. Sketch out your time blocks by type of day (e.g., weekday versus weekend) or individual days of the week. Use your model week as a guide when blocking off your schedule in your day planner or calendar management tool.

Cultivate Your Capacity

Some people prefer paper-based planners and calendars, others prefer digital, and many choose to use a hybrid system. For example, perhaps you prefer to keep a digital calendar that can be easily updated and shared with your team and family, but you also use a paper-based planner for your action planning because it helps keep you focused. Use this opportunity to revisit your system, ensure it is meeting your needs, and adjust if necessary. Here are some guiding questions as you consider whether your current calendar system meets your needs:

- **Portability:** How portable does my calendar need to be?
- **Size:** Is size a variable?
- **Schedule changes:** How frequently do my commitments shift?
- **Details:** How many details do I need to capture?
- **Formatting:** Is note formatting or space important?
- **Access:** Who else needs to have access to my schedule?
- **Plug-ins:** Are plug-ins (e.g., videoconferencing, task management tools) needed?
- **Focus:** Do I struggle with focus, particularly when using electronics?
- Are there other variables I should consider when selecting my calendar system?

To support the implementation of your model week blueprint, you may also consider labeling items on your task list with letters or highlighting them in colors that correspond to the time block in which they belong (e.g., *F* for focus-related tasks, *A* for administrative ones). This will enable you to filter key tasks for each time block and prevent you from getting sidetracked. You can also do this with tags or categories in a digital task list.

Cultivate Organizational Capacity

Assess whether the members of your team have enough time to complete their work without logging exceptionally long hours. Are they meeting too frequently throughout the week? Are meetings as focused as possible? How might you help team members thwart unnecessary distractions, particularly during focus blocks? Are they able to get into the "deep work" in their classroom or another quiet space without interruption? To explore these points, you might want to read an article I cowrote with Jill Thompson (2019) for *Educational Leadership* titled "Eight Things Teams Do to Sabotage Their Work" (www.ascd.org/el/articles/eight-things-teams-do-to-sabotage-their-work).

Tuning Techniques

Once you have established your time blocks, it is time to employ some tuning techniques to ensure that you are using them as effectively as possible. Three such techniques are filtering with fences, intentional stacking, and the Pomodoro method.

Filtering with Fences. Filters give us focus. They weed out distracting noise and allow us to home in on our priorities. Rather than feel a need to fill every inch of a calendar, focus your time by scheduling your time blocks (at their optimal time) one to three months ahead on your calendar. Then, build theoretical fences around those blocks; preserve them. You do not need to know what specific instructional planning or project you will designate in your focus block two Mondays from now, but you will allocate it to a time when your output for this task type is the strongest. When a parent emails to schedule a call or meeting, you can quickly reference the next available social block without giving away administrative time you need for copying or filing.

Former superintendent Shelley Jones-Holt shared with me the following:

> When we set boundaries for ourselves and others, we let others know that we value them, but we also value ourselves and we expect them to value themselves. What I learned was that by setting very specific times that I was available, by setting very clear expectations for those around me and by allowing other people to deal with their own issues, I freed myself to be more present for myself and my family and I was better at my position. We must set boundaries for ourselves regardless of the social constructs or contracts that we may break by doing so. Setting boundaries for ourselves and our time is critical to taking care of ourselves.

Filtering your calendar with fences gives you a more accurate sense of the volume and types of tasks you have the capacity to take on each week without pulling away your recovery or personal connection reserves. It provides greater clarity than a simple task list (or even a project-based one) and firmly distinguishes the items that get top priority within your 168-hour week. If a particular set of blocks has been filled for a given week, give yourself permission to respond in one of the following ways:

- "Yes, but not this week."
- "I may be able to take on this project, but can we review my professional priorities and team tasks together to co-identify items I may be able to let go?"
- "I don't have the capacity to take this on right now, but let's brainstorm other team members together who may be a good match."
- "No, thank you."

Guilt is a powerful force, particularly within education, and I find too many teacher and school leaders who are "voluntold" into positions they simply do not have the capacity to take on. Months later, they are burnt out and exhausted and blame it on the profession.

Pause and Reflect

Go back to your personal vision. What are you intentionally choosing? Are there positions or responsibilities you may need to let go of to free up time for the tasks that matter most in relation to your goals?

Intentional Stacking. When filling your calendar with time blocks and building fences around them, it is helpful to evaluate the timing and order of your blocks (in addition to your chronotype). Consider the following recommendations when stacking your time blocks. Set

- A recovery block for movement within 30 minutes of waking.
- Administrative blocks first and last during the workday.
- A recovery block after a focus block.
- Frequent, short recovery blocks throughout the day rather than a single long one.
- A recovery block during the "trough" of your day (based on your chronotype) when you lose energy and momentum.
- An administrative block after a social block.

Movement early in the day increases our brain function as well as offering physical benefits. As much as we might try, most of us can't resist the temptation to check email, voicemail, or social media first thing in the morning. While we may want to dive headfirst into the deep work, we most likely need to at least peek at our inbox and notifications first. Structure your schedule to allow for this; just do not get stuck there. Set a timer if you need to and stick to it.

Because they are so often overlooked, recovery blocks must be carefully tended to, especially during workday hours. Yes, you should—you must—incorporate recovery blocks into your workday. To reap optimal gains, nudge yourself to engage in a recovery block after every focus block. Try to schedule recovery blocks in shorter, more frequent bursts during the morning, when they have a greater impact, and save any afternoon recovery blocks for the escapes you most value—your preferred activities—to boost their value (Hunter & Wu, 2016).

Finally, most social blocks result in a series of next steps: meetings to be scheduled, emails to be sent, documents to be shared, and so on. By scheduling an administrative block directly after a social block, you can prevent these tasks from ever entering your action plan in the first place. Instead, they simply move from "next step" to "done."

Pause and Reflect

Revisit your model week blueprint and flag any time blocks you may want to shift to capitalize not only on your goal alignment and chronotype but also on opportunities for intentional stacking.

Pomodoro Method. Admittedly, most of us struggle most with our focus blocks. Blocking distractions and staying focused on the deep work challenges even the most intentional planners. The Pomodoro technique counteracts diversions by cycling "pomodoros"—focused 25-minute work sessions—with 5-minute breaks. After four consecutive pomodoros, individuals take a longer 15- to 30-minute break or recovery block.

The Pomodoro technique not only reduces distraction but also encourages the chunking of larger tasks into smaller, more manageable action items, creating an enhanced sense of progress. The method has become so popular that several apps are now available to time each segment and even plan for and track how many pomodoros you want to allocate to each project.

Pause and Reflect

Pause to determine whether the Pomodoro technique might be a worthwhile addition to your workflow (particularly your focus blocks).

Cultivate Your Capacity

Review the tasks you are intentionally choosing, and plan to let one position or responsibility go *per quarter* for the next year. Note these in your planner and share them with your accountability partner(s). Are there other individuals you need to inform of these likely shifts to ensure they are not caught off guard and have adequate time to plan for your replacement or changes of responsibility changes if necessary?

Update your model week blueprint to intentionally stack your time blocks where possible and practical. Look for opportunities to stack focus and recovery blocks as well as social and administrative blocks.

Download an app to support your application of the Pomodoro technique. Both the iOS and Android platforms offer a wide variety of options (free and paid) that update frequently. Search "pomodoro timer" or "focus timer" to review currently available selections. Try a few until you find one that provides the greatest motivation, then use it consistently.

Cultivate Organizational Capacity

Reflect on teacher leaders or team members who may be overstretched because, over time, they have been "voluntold" into more positions or responsibilities than they can effectively (and, more important, healthily) manage. Make time to speak with these individuals, co-identify responsibilities they may want to let go of, and co-develop a transition plan.

Review your master schedule or team schedule. Are there opportunities for more intentional stacking that you might be able to leverage for stronger team output and effectiveness?

Speak with your team about the ways they are focusing their time. If tools have proven particularly helpful for several individuals, consider how you might use professional learning resources to make them more widely accessible.

Aligning purpose with practice requires that we not only set specific and measurable goals but also structure our time to support their attainment. Now that your time has been properly allocated and distributed, we need to examine the disciplined action necessary to follow through as well as the partners and pauses that can nudge us back to center when we fall off course.

Disciplined Action

The bridge between goals and accomplishment is discipline. In the whirlwind of day-to-day chaos, you must have the focus and fortitude to stick to the plan.

Habits

Establishing strong morning, launch, shutdown, and evening rituals—collections of well-rooted habits—can anchor your days so the other components remain aligned. Our days are essentially an amalgamation of habits —coffees, workouts, showers, dog walks, commutes, and meals, among so many others. We build these habits over time and come to characterize them as "good" or "bad" within our daily routines.

The challenge is that, although we understand the importance of habits, we are often inconsistent about integrating new ones. We become overly ambitious and try to form or shift too many habits simultaneously rather than focus on strong starts and consistency. For example, at the start of a new school year, we may have lots of energy and attempt multiple new instructional strategies all at once rather than select one strategy to implement consistently for the first academic quarter before layering on a second. Forming new habits requires a minimum of 21 days of consistent action, and some habits can take as long as 254 days for full formation. Researchers have found that automaticity plateaus around 66 days after the first performance, and we should expect habit development (based on daily repetition) to take an average of 10 weeks (Gardner et al., 2012). We should focus on consistency with a small number of habits to avoid a series of false starts and stops.

Additionally, because the habits we select do not always align with our yearly or quarterly goals, they can feel like an additional burden rather than a strategy for success. If you set a goal to read more, but your habit-formation efforts focus on working out, you may end up feeling defeated quite quickly. Habits should make it easier, not harder, for you to meet your goals.

Pause and Reflect

Pause here to identify two or three habits directly aligned to your three big goals for this quarter. Though some of your goals may be achievement-oriented rather than habit-oriented, this is a good opportunity to identify new habits you might form to support your goals. Use the samples provided in the following table to guide you. What automatic actions would accelerate or enhance your goal attainment?

Sample Goal	Misaligned Habit	Aligned Habit
Read one print book and listen to one audiobook per month.	Journal every morning for 10 minutes, making note of at least one thing for which you are grateful and one thing you learned the previous day.	Read a print book for 30-45 minutes every evening Monday through Thursday. Listen to an audiobook for two hours every weekend while you fold laundry, garden, or clean.
Walk for 30 minutes at the park every weekday at 6:00 a.m.	Log your meals daily and adjust your weekly meal plan as needed.	Lay out workout clothes in the evening after brushing your teeth.

Goal-Aligned Habits

1. _____

2. _____

3. _____

Stacking

New habits form best when they are affixed to an existing positive habit. For example, you are more likely to lay out your workout clothes the night before if you sequence it directly before or after another habit you already perform consistently and with automaticity, such as brushing your teeth. You tap into an existing schema within your brain rather than fighting to rewire a completely new one.

Habits are formed (and broken) through a series of triggers and rewards. By taking an existing habit you routinely implement with consistency (and want to maintain) and stacking a new habit on top of it, you position the existing habit as a trigger for the new one. In doing so, you increase your ability to perform the new habit with the same level of consistency. Perhaps you set a goal to provide students with more consistent written feedback this quarter. You regularly review and comment on their classwork, but often forget to return the feedback to them in a timely manner. In contrast, you maintain a consistent routine for taking attendance within the first few minutes of each class period. By stacking the habit of returning student work on top of the already established attendance-taking habit, you use the existing habit as a trigger to integrate the new habit more securely. You build on your strengths.

Pause and Reflect

Pause here to identify two or three existing habits you perform consistently that you could potentially leverage as triggers for new habits you seek to form.

Existing Habits Performed Consistently		New Goal-Aligned Habits to Stack
1.	>>	
2.	>>	
3.	>>	

Breaking Bad Habits

Not all our habits are positive, and some may even hold us back from attaining our goals. To align our purpose and practice, we must look honestly at how we take disciplined action—in terms of both habit formation and habit breaking. Like habit formation, habit breaking involves a loop that includes a cue (or trigger), routine, and reward. "Over time, this loop—cue, routine, reward; cue, routine, reward—becomes more and more automatic," writes Duhigg (2014). "The cue and reward become intertwined until a powerful sense of anticipation and craving emerges" (p. 19).

To reframe bad habits, we need to take cues and rewards and replace existing (poor) routines with more positive ones. Reflect on the actions holding back or slowing down your goal attainment:

- Where are you spending too much time and getting stuck?
- What activities do you need more time to complete?
- What do you avoid?
- What makes you feel accomplished?
- What do you tend to neglect?
- Do you default to others' priorities or your own?

Perhaps one of your goals is to incorporate more movement into your daily routine, and you enjoy sitting on the couch and watching a particular TV show at 8:30 p.m. each evening. You could potentially break or refine this habit by replacing "sitting on the couch" with "riding an exercise bike" or "walking on the treadmill." You still allow yourself the opportunity to experience the reward, but only when you are in movement. The following is a simple breakdown of how this would look:

	Cue		Routine		Reward
Existing Habit	8:30 p.m.	>>	Sit on couch	>>	Watch television
New Habit	8:30 p.m.	>>	Ride or walk	>>	Watch television

Routine replacement recognizes the intertwined nature of cues and rewards—the anticipation and craving we have come to expect and enjoy over time—and shifts the behaviors we must exhibit to experience them.

Pause and Reflect

Pause here to identify a current (poor) habit loop you perform consistently and would like to refine with a more positive habit.

	Cue		Routine		Reward
Existing Habit		>>		>>	
New Habit		>>		>>	

Sticking

Over time, habits either become a regular part of our daily routine or simply fade away as failed resolutions or false starts. Our goal-aligned habits—when stacked on top of existing practice—are typically the ones that stick long-term. In addition to stacking habits and understanding the habit loop in a way that allows us to both strengthen and refine our habits, we can improve our habits' stickiness by crafting rituals at key parts of the day to increase our automaticity and, in turn, productivity.

Rituals. In his book *Free to Focus* (2019), Michael Hyatt identifies four key rituals for us to design and leverage. I have adapted them slightly for educators here:

1. *Morning Ritual*: When and how you wake, begin your day, and center yourself
2. *Launch Ritual*: Which primary professional responsibilities act as a launch pad
3. *Shutdown Ritual*: Which critical professional responsibilities get attention at day's end

4. *Evening Ritual:* When and how you slow down, recover, and reset for the next day

You may find it helpful to carve out space for each of these rituals to strengthen your habit formation and consistency over time.

Hurst-Euless-Bedford (Texas) ISD's assistant superintendent of secondary administration, Brandon Johnson, told me how daily rituals have enhanced his workflow: "I used to stare down an inbox of 680 email messages [every day]. Over time, with clarity and focus, I established a daily email goal, categorized messages into buckets, developed systems to process them efficiently, and even drafted core responses for each key category. Attacking daily challenges with clearly defined processes can help take your execution to a new level." When defining and establishing your daily rituals, consider not only the areas that have the potential to accelerate your progress but also those that are causing the most friction.

Pause and Reflect

Pause here to identify rituals that might enhance your daily routine. Where do you want to start? What part of your day needs the most support or feels the most chaotic and could benefit from additional automaticity?

Cultivate Your Capacity

Add a habit tracker to your planner or download a habit-tracking app to hold yourself personally accountable for executing your habits consistently on a weekly or daily basis. Depending on the type of habit you seek to develop, both iOS and Android provide a wide variety of habit trackers, including ones that are fully customizable by task time, type, and frequency.

Place a sticky note in the location where you perform an existing habit to remind you to stack the new one on top of it. You can even track your habit on the sticky note. Use this same strategy to remind yourself of the bad habits you seek to replace. With bad habits particularly, it can be helpful to build up to a reward or celebration for consistent replacement within the cue/trigger > routine > reward loop. Make a note of what you are working toward here for motivation.

Craft a consistent ritual for the segment of your day most in need of enhancement. Identify four to eight actions that, if sequenced and performed with greater automaticity, would increase your productivity and free you up to focus on higher-priority tasks. Use the sample rituals in Figure 2.8 to create more productive morning, launch, shutdown, and evening routines.

Cultivate Organizational Capacity
Identify organizational habits that would increase team performance. Establish a tracker to monitor performance and update it regularly. Share team progress during meetings and consistently refine your processes for improvement.

Look for opportunities to ritualize organizational meetings or routines to enhance performance. Consider designing and integrating meeting agenda templates, protocols, note-taking tools, and action plan graphic organizers to improve both efficiency and effectiveness.

Cadence of Accountability

As we look to align our purpose with our practice, the final element for us to consider is the establishment and execution of a cadence of accountability that includes partners, playbooks, and pauses. "The cadence of accountability is a rhythm of regular and frequent meetings of any team that owns a wildly important goal," write McChesney and colleagues (2016). "These meetings happen at least weekly and ideally last no more than twenty to thirty minutes. In that brief time, team members hold each other

FIGURE 2.8
Alignment Discipline in Practice: Sample Rituals

Morning Ritual

Spiritual
- [ ] Meditate.
- [ ] Practice mindfulness.
- [ ] Do yoga.
- [ ] Express gratitude.
- [ ] Pray.

Partnership
- [ ] Connect with a partner or spouse.
- [ ] Review your schedules.
- [ ] Clarify roles and needs.
- [ ] Share gratitude.
- [ ] Show support or celebrate accomplishments.

Physical
- [ ] Dress for workout.
- [ ] Drink water.
- [ ] Exercise.
- [ ] Take medicine or vitamins.
- [ ] Tend to personal grooming.

Parental
- [ ] Wake your children.
- [ ] Dress your children and/or monitor their pace.
- [ ] Prepare breakfast and/or lunches.
- [ ] Clean the dishes.
- [ ] Arrange for transportation.

Intellectual
- [ ] Scan the daily news.
- [ ] Read or listen to a book.
- [ ] Reflect on current learning.

Health
- [ ] Drink coffee or tea and/or take supplements.
- [ ] Eat breakfast.
- [ ] Log your food intake.

Launch Ritual

Social
- [ ] Greet coworkers or team members.
- [ ] Scan social media.
- [ ] Scan and stack your email inbox.
- [ ] Respond to quick emails (under 2 minutes).

Administrative
- [ ] Set your workspace.
- [ ] Review your schedule.
- [ ] Review time blocks and tasks.
- [ ] Print any necessary documents.

Focus
- [ ] Review your weekly and daily goals.
- [ ] Shift priorities if needed.
- [ ] Play music, set an oil diffuser, and minimize distractions.

Recovery
- [ ] Drink water.
- [ ] Walk and/or stretch.
- [ ] Practice mindfulness and/or review daily intentions.

(continued)

FIGURE 2.8

Alignment Discipline in Practice: Sample Rituals—(*continued*)

Shutdown Ritual

Social
- [ ] Clear your email inbox.
- [ ] Scan social media.
- [ ] Respond to notifications.
- [ ] Say goodbye to your coworkers or team.

Administrative
- [ ] Review your upcoming schedule.
- [ ] Print any necessary documents.
- [ ] Push any outstanding tasks forward.
- [ ] Reset your workspace.

Focus
- [ ] Leave "breadcrumbs" (i.e., notes or cues to oneself about where to pick up with a deep cognitive task).
- [ ] Review your weekly and daily goals.
- [ ] Shift priorities (if needed).

Recovery
- [ ] Drink water.
- [ ] Walk and/or stretch.
- [ ] Practice mindfulness and/or review daily intentions.

Evening Ritual

Spiritual
- [ ] Meditate.
- [ ] Practice mindfulness.
- [ ] Do yoga.
- [ ] Express gratitude.
- [ ] Pray.

Partnership
- [ ] Connect with your partner or spouse.
- [ ] Review your upcoming schedules.
- [ ] Clarify roles and needs.
- [ ] Express gratitude.
- [ ] Show support or celebrate accomplishments.

Physical
- [ ] Lay out your workout clothes.
- [ ] Log your water consumption.
- [ ] Complete your skincare routine.
- [ ] Take medicine or vitamins.
- [ ] Stretch.

Parental
- [ ] Help your kids with homework.
- [ ] Prepare dinner.
- [ ] Engage in evening activities (e.g., sports, music, and other extracurriculars).
- [ ] Lay out kids' clothes and pack their school and activity bags.
- [ ] Monitor kids' bedtime.

Intellectual
- [ ] Scan the daily news.
- [ ] Read or listen to a book.
- [ ] Reflect on current learning.

Health
- [ ] Drink herbal tea and/or take supplements.
- [ ] Log your food intake.
- [ ] Set your alarm for tomorrow.

accountable for producing results, despite the whirlwind" (p. 13). Together, team members provide both partnership and prompting for intentionally disciplined execution: "The magic is in the cadence. Team members must be able to hold each other accountable regularly and rhythmically. Each week, one by one, team members answer a simple question: 'What are the one or two most important things I can do in the next week (outside the whirlwind) that will have the biggest impact?'" (McChesney et al., 2016, p. 14). To plan and facilitate effective cadences of accountability, you must consider the partners, playbooks, and pauses you bring into the process.

Partners

We partner with colleagues for co-planning, book clubs, workouts, parenting advice, and even happy hours, yet somehow not for our goals. We hold goals close and may even be reluctant to share our aspirations with a trusted friend or partner. As a result, it becomes challenging to receive meaningful feedback on the goals themselves as well as to support one another in attaining them. Aligning our purpose and practice can be—but does not need to be—a solo endeavor. In the same way that you leverage structured time and disciplined action to refine your practice, a cadence of accountability can provide a respectful and mutually beneficial thought partnership.

When considering and selecting an accountability partner, lateral colleagues—those with similar experiences and goals—may be the most beneficial. (We further discuss the role of mentors—both lateral and vertical—in Chapter 3.) Lateral colleagues understand your current constraints and opportunities and share an affinity for your next moves. You might also revisit your attunement reflections from Chapter 1 (Figures 1.2 to 1.4 on pp. 21, 24, and 28) or seek out an accountability partner with a similar tendency, Enneagram, and/or type indicator to further enhance communication.

Pause and Reflect

Pause here to identify at least two individuals whom you trust who might act as accountability partners to accelerate your goal attainment. Approach these individuals to gauge their interest and follow up accordingly.

Playbooks

Once you have selected an accountability partner, you need to codevelop the playbook from which you will operate. When, where, and how will you meet? Will your connection points be synchronous or asynchronous? I have personally experienced exceptional asynchronous accountability partnerships through apps such as Voxer and other messaging tools, provided both partners were committed to the process and responded in a consistent and timely manner. Do not allow time or space to limit your potential connection points here.

During this collaboration, partners find it helpful to engage in three core areas of dialogue (McChesney et al., 2016):

1. Account: Report on last week's commitments.
2. Review: Learn from successes and failures.
3. Plan: Clear the path and make commitments.

This "playbook," if you will, can be scripted via a protocol with guiding questions to keep partners focused or evolve through organic discussion. The critical element is the commitment—to one another and to your identified actions. Partners focus on one or two of the most important commitments each one will make and deliver on in the next week.

Pause and Reflect

Before meeting with your accountability partner, consider what you might want your playbook to look and sound like. How frequently would you like to meet? How do you envision these interactions unfolding? Would a scripted, directed, or organic approach best meet your needs?

Pauses

Establishing a clear and consistent cadence of accountability not only helps educators move closer to our goals but also provides time for reflection that is so often lost amid the whirlwind of work and family obligations. By committing to one another and keeping that commitment, accountability partners offer a space for pause. These pauses recenter us on our purpose and provide an opportunity for us to assess the degree to which our current practice is aligned with our goals. Much like a quarterly retreat or end-of-year review, a cadence of accountability offers permission for us to "stop doing" so we can operate most intentionally during the 168 hours we have each week.

Pause and Reflect

Reflect on how you can leverage this cadence of accountability with your partner to establish and commit to moments of pause. How will you ensure this time remains a firm appointment on your calendar and is not overridden by lesson planning, student meetings, or grading? How will you consistently "show up" for one another?

For example, I meet with one of my accountability partners biweekly for one hour via Zoom. We have established an informal playbook of norms that ensures this time for pause and reflection is not neglected. Here are some highlights:

- The meetings are set as a recurring appointment on our calendars at a mutually agreeable time months in advance, so we schedule our work around them rather than through them.
- As part of our workday shutdown ritual the afternoon before our meeting, we often text one another to confirm we both plan to still attend. If an emergency has arisen or an appointment cannot be moved (e.g., a keynote or an important workshop for a client), the meeting is immediately rescheduled, preferably within 72 hours of the original day and time to maintain our rhythm. If we can pull off the original time without shortening our collaboration by more than 15 minutes, then we maintain our original appointment.
- We show up as we are. If it is a day when we are facilitating multiple sessions or meetings, we may log on in full professional attire. If it is a writing or creation day, we fully accept one another in sweats without makeup. We do not waste time on things that do not matter to attaining our joint goals and work together to reduce as much friction as possible.
- We establish key commitments for our next meeting and check in with each other consistently about our progress.

Cultivate Your Capacity

Send a follow-up communication to your accountability partner and set a time to establish a playbook or norms together. Consider any agenda or note-taking tools you may want to use to consistently capture and track your collaboration and progress. Block out the time you commit to on your calendars, ideally for the next three to six months, so that you schedule *around* rather than *through* this reflection time.

Cultivate Organizational Capacity

Identify how you might be able to support a cadence of accountability at the team, school, or district level. Would your staff appreciate recommendations related to accountability partner pairings? Can you provide sample agendas and/or note-taking tools to guide the process? Is there an opportunity to dedicate organizational time (20–30 minutes per week) for accountability partners to connect, reflect, and recommit?

Pause and Reflect

The integration guide in Appendix B (p. 173) brings these concepts together to guide your growth in the discipline of alignment as a purpose-driven educator. Pause here to review the integration guide and identify the next steps you will take to build your capacity in this area.

The capacity-building plan in Appendix B (p. 174) captures all the action steps for goal development, structured time, disciplined action, and cadence of accountability outlined in this chapter.

Extend the Learning Loop

The resources outlined in Figure 2.9 may provide additional support as you continue developing the discipline of alignment. Additional space has been included for you to capture your own resources for exploration as you develop a capacity-building plan for yourself and your team(s).

FIGURE 2.9
Recommended Resources: Alignment

- [ ] Berkeley Well-Being Institute Bucket List Ideas (www.berkeleywellbeing.com/bucket-list-ideas.html)
- [ ] *Free to Focus: A Total Productivity System to Achieve More by Doing Less* by Michael Hyatt (Baker, 2019)
- [ ] *Focus on This* podcast by Michael Hyatt, Megan Hyatt Miller, and company (https://focusonthispodcast.com)
- [ ] *Chop Wood Carry Water: How to Fall in Love with the Process of Becoming Great* by Joshua Medcalf (Lulu, 2015)
- [ ] *When: The Scientific Secrets of Perfect Timing* by Daniel Pink (Riverhead, 2019)
- [ ] *Internal Time: Chronotypes, Social Jet Lag, and Why You're So Tired* by Till Roenneberg (Harvard University Press, 2017)
- [ ] *Start Finishing: How to Go from Idea to Done* by Charlie Gilkey (Sounds True, 2022)
- [ ] *168 Hours: You Have More Time Than You Think* by Laura Vanderkam (Portfolio, 2011)
- [ ] *Off the Clock: Feel Less Busy While Getting More Done* by Laura Vanderkam (Portfolio, 2018)
- [ ] *Before Breakfast* podcast by Laura Vanderkam (https://lauravanderkam.com/before-breakfast-podcast)
- [ ] *The Power of Habit: Why We Do What We Do in Life and Business* by Charles Duhigg (Random House, 2014)
- [ ] *Atomic Habits: An Easy and Proven Way to Build Good Habits and Break Bad Ones* by James Clear (Avery, 2018)
- [ ] *My Morning Routine: How Successful People Start Every Day Inspired* by Benjamin Spall and Michael Xander (Portfolio, 2018)
- [ ] *Indistractable: How to Control Your Attention and Choose Your Life* by Nir Eyal (BenBella, 2019)
- [ ] *Better Than Before: Mastering the Habits of Our Everyday Lives* by Gretchen Rubin (Crown, 2015)
- [ ] *The 4 Disciplines of Execution: Achieving Your Wildly Important Goals* by Chris McChesney, Sean Covey, and Jim Huling, with Beverly Walker and Scott Thele (Simon & Schuster, 2022)
- [ ]
- [ ]
- [ ]
- [ ]

Setting clear and purpose-driven goals and exercising self-direction in our daily practice—that is to say, alignment—provides us with a clear path toward becoming who we want to be for ourselves, our families, our students, and our profession. It allows us to feel whole personally, connect with others, and experience professional progress. We cultivate school cultures grounded in recovery, belonging, and fulfillment rather than burnout. By structuring our time, taking disciplined action, and establishing a cadence of accountability, we find congruence between purpose and practice. As adult learners, we experience alignment and, in doing so, model self-management for our students.

PERSPECTIVE

It is the obvious which is so difficult to see most of
the time. People say, "It's as plain as the nose on your
face." But how much of the nose on your face can you
see, unless someone holds a mirror up to you?

—Isaac Asimov

Looking Beyond Ourselves

perspective (noun): the state of one's ideas, the facts known to one, etc., in having a meaningful interrelationship; the faculty of seeing all the relevant data in a meaningful relationship

Chapters 1 and 2 focused on how we attune our perceived and presented selves and align our purpose with our practice. In this chapter, we move beyond ourselves as singular learners to examine our learning community as a collection of individuals. Strengthening our professional and organizational capacity requires thoughtful awareness of and intentional interaction with others. But before we can engage in practices and develop norms that build toward a common good, we must create spaces that encourage safety, foster belonging, and embolden vulnerability. Cultivating safety, belonging, and vulnerability as a learning community requires members to broaden their perspective.

As you read this chapter, you can use the QR code or visit https://www .thelearningloop.com/book-perspective to access editable PDF versions of the reflection and planning tools included throughout the text. Use the case-sensitive password "StillLearning" to download the resources.

Perspective Transformation

To develop the discipline of perspective, we must engage in not only experiential learning (attunement) and self-directed learning (alignment), but also transformational learning. Perspective transformation includes three dimensions: psychological (changes in understanding of the self), convictional (revisions in belief systems), and behavioral (changes in lifestyle) (Clark, 1991).

Transformational learning involves shifting the frame of reference we use to reflect on changes in practice. For example, suppose that after collaborating with a colleague during a co-planning session, you learn of inherent inequities in many school grading systems, including, perhaps, your own (psychological dimension). As a result, you consider ways to value accelerated learning and assessment retake or revision opportunities rather than grading assignments as incomplete or zeros in your own instructional practice (convictional dimension). Finally, you begin piloting more equitable grading practices in your classroom and engage in action research to propose findings and recommendations to your school leadership team (behavioral dimension).

Early research in perspective transformation emphasized rationality and outlined the following transformation sequence:

1. Disorienting dilemma (e.g., life crisis, major transition, or accumulation of transformations)
2. Self-examination
3. Sense of alienation
4. Relating discontent to others
5. Explaining options for new behavior
6. Building confidence in new ways
7. Planning a course of action
8. Knowledge to implement plans
9. Experimenting with new roles
10. Reintegration (Mezirow, 1991, 1995)

Later theorists used neurobiological research, including brain scans during and following a dilemma period, to move beyond a sheerly rational approach and recognize the role that our emotions play in the transformational learning process. Such research stresses the importance of implicit memory, including unconscious thoughts and actions (Taylor, 1998). As we develop and strengthen the discipline of perspective, we must recognize that it demands not only a shift in schema—seeing and feeling beyond our self-view in a way that may bring discomfort—but also an openness and willingness to engage in vulnerable reflection. Only then will we experience an integrated change in behavior. In the previous example, authentic conversations about grading practices (or any challenging topic) may also mean surfacing years of misunderstandings, mistakes, and missteps. Engaging in such perspective taking requires intense levels of trust and vulnerability among team members.

Figure 3.1 provides a capacity-building blueprint for developing and strengthening one's perspective discipline. You will notice that this blueprint, unlike those in the previous two chapters, includes both organizational and individual commitments and outcomes. While one can certainly develop the discipline of perspective as an individual, such growth is accelerated and deepened in organizations committed to both skill building and culture tending.

FIGURE 3.1

Capacity-Building Blueprint: Perspective

Shift in Schema and Reflection That Leads to Integrated Change in Behavior			
Organizational Commitment	*Organizational Commitment*		*Organizational Outcome*
Build Safety and Foster Belonging	**Embolden Vulnerability**	**=**	**Learning Community Connected Through Shared Experience**
Individual Commitment	*Individual Commitment*		*Individual Outcome*
Catalyze a Shift in Schema	**Make Space for Reflection**		**Integrated Change in Behavior**

Organizational Commitment

Unlike attunement and alignment, perspective is not a solo act but, rather, a social one. Educators gain and broaden their perspective when they actively and intentionally engage with other professionals within their organization —whether that organization is a team, a school, or a system. Such capacity building requires individuals to shift their schema and make space for reflection. However, for this to occur, there must also be an organizational commitment—at least on a small scale (i.e., at the team level)—to build safety, foster belonging, and embolden vulnerability.

Build Safety

The Whole School, Whole Community, Whole Child model acknowledges the importance of safety as a key tenet of both student and employee wellness. Beyond physical safety, we need to ensure that both adults and students feel a sense of emotional safety within our schools. In *The Culture Code* (2018a), Daniel Coyle outlines steps leaders can take to cultivate safe spaces. A few of these steps are highlighted here with ideas for what they may look like within a school context. However, Coyle notes, it is important to recognize that

> building safety isn't the kind of skill you can learn in a robotic, paint-by-numbers sort of way. It's a fluid, improvisational skill—sort of like learning to pass a soccer ball to a teammate during a game. It requires you to recognize patterns, react quickly, and deliver the right signal at the right time. And like any skill, it comes with a learning curve. (p. 74)

The perspective reflection at the end of this section provides you with an opportunity to consider how you might further cultivate your team, school, or district as a safe space for all members.

Spotlight Your Fallibility Early On (Coyle, 2018a, p. 75). Having coached educators for several years, I've noticed that many believe they must have *all* the answers—that as teachers and leaders, they need to project infallibility to demonstrate strength. If anything, this develops an unrealistic (and unhealthy) expectation that failure and growth do not have a place in our learning organizations, when in reality quite the opposite is true. Our communities thrive on mistakes, or faithful (not just first) attempts in learning (i.e., F.A.I.L.—an acronym usually credited to former president of India A. P. J. Abdul Kalam). Such growth points impact how we continue to stretch as a living, breathing ecosystem.

Educators have a responsibility not only to embrace their mistakes, but also to highlight them. Ensure you send a clear message: "This is how we work here. We do not grow through perfection, but through persistence and progress." When mistakes are made, particularly those that affect the community, own them. Step into them. Then, in a solutions-oriented manner, outline your next steps and request others' support and input. This models for others that gaining perspective can also sometimes mean responding incorrectly. The possibility (or even certainty) of making mistakes should not mean that we avoid perspective taking but, rather, that we embrace it.

Embrace the Messenger (Coyle, 2018a, p. 75). It is 5:00 p.m. You are responding to your final emails and phone calls before packing your bag, and a colleague enters your office or classroom to share concerns. In these circumstances, it is easy to deflect or become defensive. As leaders (for both our staff members and students), we have a responsibility both to see the big picture (or take a "balcony view") *and* to understand individual needs from down on the dance floor (Heifetz et al., 2009). Just because we do not like what we see doesn't mean we can ignore it. When members of our learning community operate with courage and vulnerability to transparently share feedback and ideas, this is a signal for us to lean in rather than pull back. Embracing our messengers, particularly when we do not like the message, establishes a culture in which others feel safe, demonstrates a willingness to engage, and helps us determine whether both staff member and student voice are truly valued.

If you are unable to fully engage in the present moment, be honest. Request that you connect tomorrow or the next day when you can commit to hear both the messenger and the message in a focused, positive, and solution-oriented manner. When we deflect, we also deflate.

Create Safe, Collision-Rich Spaces (Coyle, 2018a, p. 81). Teaching can be an incredibly isolating profession. Do whatever you can, as both a leader and a teacher, to draw people closer. Cook food, host contests, celebrate small wins, buy a nicer coffee machine, invest in a ping-pong table, play human-sized Hungry Hungry Hippo, stand on your head (and yes, I have witnessed all of these). It is worth it. We often view staff lounges as grounds for gossip and overlook that they're also fertile soil for connection and perspective taking.

Coyle (2018a) notes that collisions act as the "lifeblood of any organization, the key driver of creativity, community, and cohesion" (p. 66). Educators must recognize that their facilitative role expands beyond *model* to include *architect*. Get people close together within visual contact of one another.

Coyle cites MIT professor Thomas Allen, who found that individuals demonstrate the strongest social connections when they work less than eight meters apart—what is known as the Allen Curve. At less than six meters, communication skyrockets, and at more than 50 meters, it ceases. "In other words, proximity functions as a kind of connective drug," Coyle (2018a) writes. "Get close, and our tendency to connect lights up" (p. 71).

These connections improve not only communication but also productivity. Do what you can to orchestrate meaningful gatherings, not just meetings. (See Priya Parker's work on "the art of gathering" at www.priyaparker.com for additional context and ideas.)

Make Sure Everyone Has a Voice (Coyle, 2018a, p. 81). Learner voice—for both students and staff members—may be one of the most over-touted and underrealized values in our school vision and mission statements. We recognize its importance, and we seek to give learners a voice. We may even administer regular surveys and facilitate focus groups or one-on-one meetings to collect data. The question becomes, "What do we do with the knowledge we gather?" Are these pieces of information heard and acted upon? If not, how do we reflect the reasons why back to our community members? These actions (or, in many cases, inactions) matter.

Russell Quaglia and Lisa Lande (2017) outline key components of teacher voice that are relevant for educators across our systems. "Teacher voice is about *listening* to others, *learning* from what is being said, and *leading* by taking action together," they write. "When [it is] used effectively, teachers listen at least as often as they speak, put more energy into learning than trying to convince others, and lead by taking action with the best interest of all concerned in mind" (p. 79). In this way, perspective taking goes beyond hearing one another to acting together.

Capitalize on Threshold Moments (Coyle, 2018a, p. 84). As noted in Chapter 2, beginnings matter. Threshold moments within our school cultures such as new employee onboarding, the first day of staff professional learning, first day of school, and start of each school day offer culture-building opportunities. Use the appeal of these fresh starts not to peddle another "flavor of the month" but, instead, to set and define moments of arrival. Our brains make decisions at the start of each event about *whether* and *how* to connect, and there is opportunity here to ensure that all feel welcome. Do not miss these proverbial and psychological threshold moments.

Pause and Reflect

Pause here to reflect on and respond to the prompts in Figure 3.2. Note that nonexamples or missteps can, at times, provide us with even stronger insight than the "right" way of doing things. Push yourself to identify moments in each of the action areas you now view as growth opportunities. Consider how you might respond differently in the future.

Cultivate Your Capacity

Identify one growth opportunity from your reflection, review the next steps and considerations you identified, and take action to refine your practice in this area. Consider sharing these action steps with the accountability partner(s) you identified in Chapter 2, and include them as part of your weekly commitments.

Cultivate Organizational Capacity

Set up the actions for building safe spaces as a gallery walk in an upcoming staff or team meeting. Write each action at the top of a sheet of chart paper positioned at different points around the room. For the first two actions—"spotlight fallibility early on" and "embrace the messenger"—invite staff members to identify individuals who exhibit these actions exceptionally well and could be models for others. For the remaining three actions, ask staff members how we might better leverage our environment, mechanisms for input, and starting points to build spaces in which all members feel safe.

FIGURE 3.2

Perspective Reflection: Build Safety

Actions for Building Safe Spaces	Growth Opportunities	Next Steps and Considerations
Spotlight Your Fallibility Early On Identify a time when you felt a need to conceal a professional mistake or poor decision you made. Who did you hide it from and why?		
Embrace the Messenger Reflect on an interaction in which you deflected the message/messenger and became defensive. What may have triggered this reaction? What feelings did it evoke?		
Create Safe, Collision-Rich Spaces Consider ways in which you may have distanced others (or distanced yourself from others). How might you act not only as a model but also an architect for connection and cohesion?		
Make Sure Everyone Has a Voice Note an example in which you solicited input, but it was not truly heard or acted upon. What made you decide to ignore it? Why?		
Capitalize on Threshold Moments Select an event that members of your learning community might identify as a threshold moment. In what ways could you better use this opportunity for connection and perspective taking?		

The italicized actions for building safe spaces come from D. Coyle, 2018, *The culture code: The secrets of highly successful groups* (pp. 75, 81, & 84), Bantam Books.

Foster Belonging

A sense of belonging is situated in the middle of Maslow's hierarchy of needs for good reason. Our physiological and safety needs must be met first, but both belonging and esteem are still considered deficiency needs—that is, needs that must be tended to before our growth needs or self-actualization/fulfillment can be achieved. All individuals have a need to feel safe and a desire to feel as though we belong. Within the workplace, we tend to misconstrue the concept of belonging as merely "teaming" or "partnering." It is not enough to bring people together or even to orchestrate collision-rich spaces in which they organically cohere with one another. Although these communication points breed safety, they do not consequently cultivate belonging. A true sense of belonging requires intentional and varied connections, especially as we collectively work to create and sustain learning communities that value inclusion.

Inclusion. Although many districts still have far to go in their recruitment and retention of a diverse workforce at all levels of the system, steps continue to be taken during the marketing, interviewing, and hiring phases to diversify staff. This, in turn, offers a diversity of perspectives not only for our teams but, ultimately, for our students as well. However, staff inclusion and belonging does not stop at the hiring gate. "Belonging isn't the same as joining in," write Jacob and colleagues (2020, p. 44). "The joiners-in are the easy ones to give a sense of Belonging to. Great Belonging culture includes the outsiders, the geeks, the introverts, the alphas and the betas, the extroverts and the confident, the nervous and the timid, the optimistic and the anxious. And it gives each person who can contribute what they need and a reason to belong."

As we look to foster cultures of inclusion in which everyone experiences a sense of belonging, mentoring serves a critical role. The education profession does not take this role seriously enough. We focus on logging frequent connection points, much like professional development seat time, rather than on more closely examining interaction quality. Too often, I hear of instructional coaches tightly bound by formulaic cycles and rigid weekly or biweekly meeting schedules rather than flexibly designed models to provide "just in time" coaching immediately to the educators who need it most in their moments of greatest need. As a result, our mentoring or coaching skims the surface, causing some shifts in instructional approaches but not resulting in sustained and integrated changes in practice. While we need consistent points of contact with our mentors, it is equally important that these connections transpire when we are ready and that we not feel rushed between instructional blocks and bells. Coyle (2018a) recommends "flash mentoring" (p. 166). Pick someone you want to learn from and shadow them—but for hours instead of months or years. This sense of urgency breaks down barriers and helps build connections faster.

Another approach considers varied categories of mentorship—not just a single partnership—to ensure that all new members of our learning community are intentionally paired with individuals who serve different purposes. In Chapter 2, I mentioned the importance of both lateral (or peer-to-peer) and vertical mentors. We break down the "Glass Slipper Syndrome" (Jacob et al., 2020), where individuals only pretend to fit in, by creating cultures where individuals engage in mentorships that strategically and thoughtfully build belonging, such as by taking on the following roles:

- A sponsor—Someone who talks you up when you're not there
- A wing-[person]—Someone who helps you in ways you cannot help yourself
- A cheerleader—[Someone who] cheers you on, no matter what
- An ally from the "other side"—Someone from another "cohort" who will provide unexpected support
- The buddy—Cheers you up, laughs with you, mops you up, has a good moan with you (Jacob et al., 2020, p. 130)

Mentor programs and pairings need to focus on the *people* dynamics—who we match and why—as much as the *process* ones (e.g., frequency of meetings, recommended activities, learning logs). Connecting individuals on the same grade-level teams or in the same content areas promotes knowledge-based collaboration, but it does not necessarily foster a culture of belonging. We have a responsibility to find ways to better leverage relationships within our school communities.

Cultivate Organizational Capacity

Begin with yourself. Pause here to identify your own mentors, ideally within your school community. Do you have individuals you can turn to who fill these different roles for you? If not, whom might you seek out? Use Figure 3.3 as a brainstorming space to guide your next steps.

FIGURE 3.3

Perspective Reflection: Foster Belonging

Mentor Type	Individual -OR- Ideas for Connection
Sponsor—Someone who talks you up when you're not there	
Wing-[person]—Someone who helps you in ways you cannot help yourself	
Cheerleader—[Someone who] cheers you on, no matter what	
Ally from the "other side"—Someone from another "cohort" who will provide unexpected support	
Buddy—Someone who cheers you up, laughs with you, mops you up, has a good moan with you	

Descriptions of mentor types come from K. Jacob, S. Unerman, & M. Edwards, 2020, *Belonging: The key to transforming and maintaining diversity, inclusion, and equality at work* (p. 130), Bloomsbury.

Cultivate Your Capacity

Select one "idea for connection" from your reflection and make a commitment to connect with that individual within the next month. Schedule an initial 20- to 30-minute mentoring meeting in which you outline how they may be able to support your growth, inviting input from their experience. Consider grabbing coffee or sharing lunch at school together. Then, within the next three months, commit to a longer collaboration period (at least two hours) in which you will engage in a flash mentoring session. Set clear outcomes and an agenda for this time to make it as intentional and meaningful as possible. Later, pay it forward with your own mentee.

Cultivate Organizational Capacity

Consider how you might use the mentor categories in your onboarding and staff growth processes. Are there staff members you can match now to foster belonging? What systems and structures might you put in place to facilitate and support such connections in the future? Are there adjustments and refinements you can make to your coaching program and protocols to improve the quality of collaboration and accelerate growth—not just when it is scheduled, but when it is needed?

Individual Commitment

When organizations build safety and foster belonging, it broadens educators' perspectives (i.e., social awareness) and creates a learning community connected through shared experience. Professionals who have opportunities to meaningfully connect with one another, and feel safe doing so, can transform their perspective through shifts in schema. They move beyond recycling old practices (e.g., outdated hiring and grading policies, learning activities, and procedures and routines) and instead engage in continuous cycles of growth together. However, just because an educator works in an organization committed to safety and belonging does not mean such behavioral change will automatically occur. It requires an individual commitment and willingness to shift one's schema (or old practices) as well.

Catalyze a Shift in Schema

Psychological research shows that perspective transformation at the individual level begins with a disorienting dilemma (Mezirow, 1978). Although educators may not always have a disorienting dilemma such as a life crisis, major transition, or accumulation of transformations triggering a shift in schema, we do have an obligation to engage in perspective taking to build more engaged and productive learning communities. To do so, we must recognize the differences among transmissional, transactional, and transformational learning. In transmissional learning, information passes from one individual to another. In essence, we say to the other person, "I see you." In transactional learning, we account for one another's experiences and may even engage in critical thinking together. We validate each other's perspective: "I value you." Transformational learning, however, moves beyond recognition and value to prompt a shift in our own behavior. We are willing to question or reorder how we previously thought or acted (Brookfield, 2000). Engaging in such vulnerable reflection requires us to be aware and critical of our assumptions as well as to recognize our own frames of reference. We can only do this in professional spaces where we feel a sense of safety and belonging. This culture building begins with leaders but must be owned and sustained by all members of our learning communities.

Over time, it is not uncommon for educators at all levels of the system to become stuck in their practice and resistant to change. Often this is not a symptom of stubbornness or unprofessionalism as much as it is a sign of exhaustion. Educators are, quite simply, tired. Schemas act as a cognitive framework to help us organize information both personally and professionally. They enable us to process information more efficiently, but they can also filter out critical elements. As educators, we utilize schemas for tasks such as unit and lesson planning, assessment design, and feedback and grading practices. These schemas become refined over time through research, implementation, peer collaboration, and student input. As these frameworks are more firmly positioned, it becomes more challenging to shift them.

Building safety and fostering belonging creates space for educators to engage in dialogue that challenges existing schemas. Safety and belonging at the organizational level create less friction for individuals to shift their own schemas and those of others. However, even if a team, school, or district is still developing its organizational culture, there are steps individuals can take to create a disorienting dilemma, invite productive conversations, and promote shifts in practice.

Cultivate Your Capacity

Collect a classroom-based data set that prompts a disorienting dilemma or sets up a disconnect between existing and possible practice. For example, you may wonder if providing students with feedback *and* a grade simultaneously affects the degree to which they process and respond to feedback in their revisions. Perhaps you try offering feedback first, without the grade, to see if it results in a stronger student response to revision. Try to remain as objective as possible in your data collection, particularly if/when it does not match up to the findings you may have expected. Use the data to engage in a one-on-one conversation with an accountability partner or team member. Identify trends you anticipated as well as those you did not and seek possible causes together. Draft two or three prompts you will use to capture additional insights consistently over the next few weeks, then meet again to share findings.

Cultivate Organizational Capacity

Find or collect a data set that prompts a disorienting dilemma or sets up an intentional disconnect between existing practice and possible practice. This could be a research study, school- or districtwide data you collect and analyze, or classroom data you collect and act upon. As much as possible, the data should be objective in nature. Use protocols to structure and facilitate productive conversations. These could be one-on-one or team-based but should have a defined starting point and outcomes established at the onset. The National School Reform Faculty offers a wide range of free protocols to guide this work at https://nsrfharmony.org/protocols. You may also find the guidance and protocols included in the following books helpful in your planning and facilitation:

- *Protocols for Professional Learning* (2009) by Lois Brown Easton
- *Facilitating Teacher Teams and Authentic PLCs: The Human Side of Leading People, Protocols, and Practices* (2018) by Daniel Venables
- *Intentional Moves: How Skillful Leaders Impact Learning* (2023) by Elisa B. MacDonald

Embed the key action steps from these conversations into reflection tools for team members to capture ways in which they may be seeing circumstances or events from a different perspective.

Organizational Commitment

Beyond building safety and fostering belonging, organizations must commit to emboldening vulnerability—encouraging colleagues to openly share their growth opportunities and areas where they might need communal support.

Embolden Vulnerability

Within the context of perspective transformation, the decision to be vulnerable—in both our reflection and subsequent behavioral changes—is a solo act. However, much as there are actions we can take as a learning community to breed safety and belonging, there are also moves we can make to promote vulnerability as both an acceptable and encouraged professional practice. "Building habits of group vulnerability is like building a muscle," writes Coyle (2018a). "It takes time, repetition, and the willingness to feel pain in order to achieve gains" (p. 158). In our conversation, educator Michael Crawford highlighted the importance of this approach within our school communities: "In the past I often plowed ahead without really hearing others. As a result, I missed opportunities to learn about who I was and could have been, and I failed to appreciate others in real and deep ways.

When teams walk the talk of vulnerability, they see others for who they are, make them feel safe, and invite them to be their fullest selves."

The following are some ways we can "walk the talk" and embolden vulnerability in our schools.

Be Vulnerable First and Often (Coyle, 2018a, p, 158). In the same way educators spotlight their fallibility early to establish a sense of safety, leaders should be vulnerable first and often. This runs against the grain of school environments that look to leaders as strong and unruffled. Vulnerability equates not to a lack of confidence, but instead to a willingness to lay feelings bare. "Are we about appearing strong or about exploring the landscape together?" asks Coyle (2018a). "Are we about winning interactions, or about learning together?" (p. 161).

Pause and Reflect

Brené Brown offers guiding questions to learn about the culture and values of a group, particularly as it relates to vulnerability. Pause here and use Figure 3.4 as a space to consider how Brown's questions apply to your team, school, or district's strengths and growth opportunities. To what degree do team members open themselves up to be vulnerable with one another?

Harvard organizational behaviorist Jeff Polzer recommends that we focus on two critical moments when forming new groups: the first vulnerability and the first disagreement. Vulnerability is

> about sending a really clear signal that you have weaknesses, that you could use help. And if that behavior becomes a model for others, then you can set the insecurities aside and get to work, start to trust each other and help each other. If you never have that vulnerable moment, on the other hand, then people will try to cover up their weaknesses, and every little micro-task becomes a place where insecurities manifest themselves. (quoted in Coyle, 2018b, p. 1)

FIGURE 3.4

Perspective Reflection: Embolden Vulnerability

Guiding Question	Strengths	Growth Opportunities
What behaviors are rewarded? Punished?		
Where and how are people actually spending their resources (time, money, attention)?		
What rules and expectations are followed, enforced, and ignored?		
Do people feel safe and supported talking about how they feel and asking for what they need?		
What are the sacred cows? Who is most likely to tip them? Who stands the cows back up?		
What stories are legend and what values do they convey?		
What happens when someone fails, disappoints, or makes a mistake?		
How is vulnerability (uncertainty, risk, and emotional exposure) perceived?		
How prevalent are shame and blame, and how are they showing up?		
What's the collective tolerance for discomfort? Is the discomfort of learning, trying new things, and giving and receiving feedback normalized, or is there a high premium put on comfort (and how does that look)?		

Guiding questions come from B. Brown, 2012, *Daring greatly: How the courage to be vulnerable transforms the way we live, love, parent, and lead* (p. 174), Avery.

When a leader demonstrates vulnerability, the second person, or responder, is critical. These shared exchanges, or vulnerability loops, establish norms and ultimately develop a culture of trust or distrust (Coyle, 2018b). Following are strategies for developing and sustaining vulnerability loops between the individual who first demonstrates vulnerability and the responder.

Listen Like a Trampoline. As responders, we can improve our listening skills and strengthen our exchanges by listening like a trampoline, Zenger and Folkman (2016) suggest. Strong listeners, they write, are those "you can bounce ideas off of—and rather than absorbing your ideas and energy, they amplify, energize, and clarify your thinking. They make you feel better not merely by passively absorbing, but actively supporting. This lets you gain energy and height, just like someone jumping on a trampoline" (p. 4). When listening, reflection that leads to perspective transformation involves more than remaining silent, exhibiting facial expressions and verbal affirmations, and being able to repeat what others have said. Good listening means a true dialogue and cooperative conversation.

Cultivate Your Capacity

Hone your craft as a listener and responder. In an upcoming dialogue with a trusted peer, ask if you can audio-record the conversation for your own self-reflection. Use a transcription app such as Otter (https://otter.ai) to provide you with a transcript for deeper and more targeted reflection. Note areas where you listened and responded versus those where you truly amplified what was said. Is there a pattern to how you begin your responses or reflection points or transition back to the speaker? What energy-giving practices can you replicate and expand? Which deflating ones should you avoid and replace?

Cultivate Organizational Capacity

While emboldening vulnerability begins at the peer-to-peer level, it is truly tested at the team level. Who is first on the court when challenging conversations arise? Who is catching the ball? Who is passing with purpose? Teams may find it helpful to video-record co-planning meetings, professional learning communities, or other collaborative gatherings to develop a stronger understanding of the flow of communication and ways it could be refined. Platforms such as Sibme (https://sibme.com) make it seamless to simultaneously share these conversations with both a coach and teammates. Such platforms also provide space for teams to establish collective norms for communication and make note of strengths, growth opportunities, and ideas related to each of the norms or practices in the video. In this way, emboldening vulnerability becomes both transparent and celebrated as a worthwhile practice.

Nurture Candor-Generating Practices (Coyle, 2018a, p. 164). High-performing organizations, including schools, operate with open and transparent dialogue and have systems, models, and protocols that support and encourage such transparency. These concepts are examined in greater depth in Chapter 5, where we explore the discipline of organizational learning, but it is important to highlight a few candor-generating practices here, particularly as we look to nurture vulnerability in our spaces.

• **After-action reviews.** According to Darling and colleagues (2005), after-action reviews (AARs) are used by the U.S. Army to extract lessons from events or projects, and similar reviews have been used by large corporations to identify both best practices and mistakes to avoid. They act as more than a postmortem in that they examine not only *what to do* but also *how to think*. An effective AAR addresses four key questions:

1. "What were our intended results?
2. "What were our actual results?
3. "What caused our results?
4. "What will we sustain or improve?" (Darling et al., 2005)

School teams might integrate AARs following a significant performance-based student assessment, benchmark assessment, or parent and community engagement event.

Cultivate Organizational Capacity

Additional information about AARs is available in the *Harvard Business Review* article "Learning in the Thick of It" by Darling and colleagues, available here: https://hbr.org/2005/07/learning-in-the-thick-of-it.

• **"The Braintrust" and solution groups.** According to Ed Catmull (2014), cofounder of Pixar, Pixar uses a process it calls "the Braintrust" every few months to provide a mechanism for candid feedback throughout the creative process of film generation. Much like the passion-driven field of education, the work of creative artists can require an iterative process of consistent reworking. At Pixar, the Braintrust acts as a space for people to hear one another's "notes," put positions and authority aside, and focus on identifying problems and generating solutions. As with AARs, the Braintrust at Pixar focuses on actions rather than a singular individual. This kind of solution group provides clarity by gathering individuals who have a vested interest in one another's success. It is distinguished from other feedback mechanisms in that it includes individuals who have a deep understanding of and commitment to the craft (in Pixar's case, storytelling) and eliminate any dynamics of authority.

At Pixar, Catmull noted, in addition to the formally established Braintrust for each film, individuals are encouraged to create their own solution groups. Andrew Stanton recommends the following qualifications for members of a solution group: "The people you choose must (a) make you think smarter and (b) put lots of solutions on the table in a short amount of time. I don't care who it is, the janitor or the intern or one of your most-trusted lieutenants: If they can help you do that, they should be at the table" (quoted in Catmull, 2014, para. 29). To this end, Catmull (2014) continues, you should "seek out people who are willing to level with you, and when you find them, hold them close" (para. 30). School teams might develop their own solution groups when presenting and reviewing strategic goals, considering new or adapted instructional approaches, or evaluating the effectiveness of strategies or assessments (during both the planning and implementation phases).

Pause and Reflect

Pause here to read more about Pixar's Braintrust in Ed Catmull's 2014 *Fast Company* article, "Inside the Pixar Braintrust": www.fastcompany .com/3027135/inside-the-pixar-braintrust.

Cultivate Organizational Capacity

Brainstorm how you might use AARs or solution groups to nurture candor-generating practices within your team, school, or district. How can these collaborative structures be leveraged to embolden vulnerability and, ultimately, deepen reflective practice?

• **Establish boundaries between performance reviews and professional learning.** Though performance reviews and professional learning both play an important role in adult development, they hold different roles and functions (Coyle, 2018a). A performance review represents an endpoint, a summative assessment of where we have landed and what we have accomplished (or may still be developing). By contrast, professional learning, when strategically designed and facilitated, is more self-directed than system-directed. It values the learner as a goal-setter, co-creator, and social constructor (Rodman, 2019). When we conflate performance reviews and professional learning, we perpetuate organizational cultures that not only stagnate growth but also stunt it.

We need to establish clear boundaries between performance reviews and professional learning at all levels of the educational system. Our focus should be on professional learning, or formative growth, rather than summative performance. How committed is an individual to promoting organizational development through productive team dialogue and practice sharing? To what degree have they engaged in learning opportunities both inside and beyond the organization to stretch their practice and strengthen team performance?

While I support clearly aligning professional learning opportunities to targets and performance indicators within our evaluative frameworks, we must also allow space for learning in its raw, unfiltered, and uncensored state. If staff members engage in meaningful, authentic dialogue but you cannot directly tie it to a growth target, step back and let it go. The true work of education requires both innovation and vulnerability, for which productive spaces are needed.

Individual Commitment

Once a shift in our individual schema(s) has occurred, individuals adept in the discipline of perspective make space for reflection. They step back to determine which shifts they will reject and which will become an integrated change in their behavior.

Make Space for Reflection

Before our behaviors can change, we need to be able to reflect on them. Reflection, particularly for those of us who position ourselves deeply in our work, is both beautiful and messy. It opens a window to our strengths—the practices we refine and continue to replicate—but also holds a mirror to our scars and blemishes—the mistakes we have made in the past but have not fully grown through, as well as new challenges we are still working to overcome.

When I transitioned from instructional coach to school leader, deep and consistent reflection was one of the most challenging skills for me to hone. In hindsight, I feel this is because we tend to exclusively equate reflection with the activity of writing or journaling. But for many, this is not the most accessible entry point to reflection. As I grew, I learned that reflection could manifest in the forms of thought partners, masterminds, professional learning networks, and accountability relationships. It could also develop through mindful breathing, intentional pauses in my workflow, and regular stretching and yoga. These communication and movement patterns provided the reflection necessary for my continued growth. I now frequently journal, but it has taken significant habit formation and experimentation with the right prompts (not just a blank page) to lead me to this point. I mention this because it is naïve of us to value reflective practice and make sweeping claims that all educators should pause and journal without recognizing the varied (and valuable) ways in which this action surfaces differently for individuals. Reflection marks an act of vulnerability, and the reality is that some of us are more comfortable in bare conversations than blank pages. Those who have experienced similar challenges may find the following collections of prompts helpful:

- For daily focus: *Navigating the Chaos: 365 Questions to Ask Yourself on the Art of Living* (2021), by Michael Edmondson*
- For weekly focus: *Friday Forward: Inspiration and Motivation to End Your Week Stronger Than It Started* (2021), Robert Glazer
- For monthly focus: *Onward: Cultivating Emotional Resilience in Educators* (2018), by Elena Aguilar

Outcomes of Perspective Taking

Building safety, fostering belonging, and emboldening vulnerability at the organizational level creates a learning community connected through shared experience. Over time, spotlighting our fallibilities, embracing feedback from one another, amplifying others' voices, and promoting inclusivity through varied mentorships provides a strong foundation upon which individuals can see and be seen. Our willingness to be vulnerable, paired with responsive listening and candor-generating practices, crafts a shared

---

*On a personal note, Michael Edmondson is my former high school social studies teacher—an individual who marked up my papers more than any other teacher I have known since. I cannot tell you how many times I heard his voice telling me to "use the active voice" as I wrote this manuscript. When he signed my copy of *Navigating the Chaos,* he wrote, "Like us, this book is a work in progress," and I could not agree more.

experience through which we not only connect but also learn and grow. We feel comfortable challenging the status quo, taking new perspectives, and considering shifts in our schemas—even those that are firmly established. When we make space for reflection at both the individual and organizational levels, we experience integrated changes across the system.

Pause and Reflect

The integration guide in Appendix C (p. 177) brings the concepts in this chapter together to guide your individual and organizational growth in the discipline of perspective. Pause here to review the integration guide and identify the next steps you will take to build your capacity in this area.

The capacity-building plan in Appendix C (p. 178) captures all the action steps for reflection, cultivating your capacity, and cultivating organizational capacity outlined in this chapter.

Extend the Learning Loop

The resources outlined in Figure 3.5 may provide additional support as you continue developing the discipline of perspective. Additional space has been included for you to capture your own resources for exploration as you develop a capacity-building plan for yourself and your team(s).

In Chapter 4, we explore how trustworthy communities and a focus on continuous growth create deliberately developmental organizations rooted in collective efficacy. In this way, we move beyond perspective to define not only *what we do* as a learning community but *how we do it*.

FIGURE 3.5

Recommended Resources: Perspective

☐ *The Culture Code: The Secrets of Highly Successful Groups* by Daniel Coyle (Random House, 2019)

☐ "How Showing Vulnerability Builds a Stronger Team" by TED Ideas, Daniel Coyle (https://ideas.ted.com/how-showing-vulnerability-helps-build-a-stronger-team)

☐ *The Art of Gathering* by Priya Parker (Riverhead, 2020)

☐ *Teacher Voice: Amplifying Success* by Russell Quaglia and Lisa Lande (Corwin, 2017)

☐ *Belonging: The Key to Transforming and Maintaining Diversity, Inclusion and Equality at Work* by Kathryn Jacob, Sue Unerman, and Mark Edwards (Bloomsbury, 2022)

☐ National School Reform Faculty Protocols (https://nsrfharmony.org/protocols)

☐ *Protocols for Professional Learning* by Lois Brown Easton (ASCD, 2009)

☐ *Facilitating Teacher Teams and Authentic PLCs: The Human Side of Leading People, Protocols, and Practices* by Daniel R. Venables (ASCD, 2018)

☐ *Daring Greatly: How the Courage to Be Vulnerable Transforms the Way We Live, Love, Parent, and Lead* by Brené Brown (Avery, 2012)

☐ TED Talk on "The Power of Vulnerability" by Brené Brown (www.ted.com/talks/brene_brown_the_power_of_vulnerability)

☐ "Learning in the Thick of It," in *Harvard Business Review,* by Marilyn Darling, Charles Parry, and Joseph Moore (2005) (https://hbr.org/2005/07/learning-in-the-thick-of-it)

☐ "Inside the Pixar Braintrust," in *Fast Company,* by Ed Catmull (2014) (www.fastcompany.com/3027135/inside-the-pixar-braintrust)

☐ *Navigate the Chaos: 365 Questions to Ask Yourself on the Art of Living* by Michael Edmondson (Lulu.com, 2020)

☐ *Friday Forward: Inspiration and Motivation to End Your Week Stronger Than It Started* by Robert Glazer (Simple Truths, 2021)

☐

☐

☐

☐

4

COLLECTIVE EFFICACY

If I have the belief that I can do it,
I shall surely acquire the capacity to do it even
if I may not have it at the beginning.

—Mahatma Gandhi

Becoming a Deliberately Developmental Organization

collective (adjective): forming a whole; combined; of or characteristic of a group of individuals taken together

efficacy (noun): capacity for producing a desired result or effect; effectiveness

We define schools through a variety of metrics: enrollment, student achievement, student growth, teacher/leader quality, teacher retention, family engagement, building size, population diversity—the list goes on. Yet despite all these measures, we often fail to recognize that schools are, in essence, developmental organizations. They are spaces that consider and value not only organizational potential, but also human potential. The strongest organizations—in education as well as business—do more than *leverage* organizational and human capacity; they are intentional about *building* it. They recognize that in an increasingly volatile, uncertain, complex, and ambiguous (VUCA) world, we must foster adaptive skills even more than technical ones. "Research shows that the single biggest cause of work burnout is not work overload," write Kegan and Laskow Lahey (2016), "but working too long without experiencing your own personal development" (p. 10). We need to grow our people.

This chapter revisits the concept of self-efficacy but this time as situated within the broader scope of the developmental organization, whether it's a district, school, or team. We delve into how developing the discipline of collective efficacy—our shared belief that we can accomplish our goals—produces both stronger organizations and flourishing team members. When we establish trustworthy communities focused on continuous growth, we become deliberately developmental organizations that can easily adapt rather than burn out when faced with changing and complex needs. Figure 4.1 provides a collective efficacy blueprint to guide your exploration of this discipline.

> As you read this chapter, you can use the QR code or visit https://www
> .thelearningloop.com/book-collective-efficacy to access editable PDF
> versions of the reflection and planning tools included throughout the
> text. Use the case-sensitive password "StillLearning" to download the
> resources.

FIGURE 4.1

Capacity-Building Blueprint: Collective Efficacy

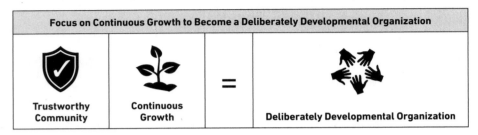

Focus on Continuous Growth to Become a Deliberately Developmental Organization			
Trustworthy Community	Continuous Growth	=	Deliberately Developmental Organization

Understanding Self-Efficacy

In Chapter 2, we examined the importance of self-efficacy as it relates to goal achievement. Our belief in whether we can execute a plan of action impacts our outcomes (Bandura, 1977). Daily affirmations, motivational quotes, and pep talks do more than make us feel inspired: When we internalize those messages—and believe in our ability to accomplish the goals we set—we increase the likelihood we will achieve them.

Psychologists use a variety of tools to measure individuals' self-efficacy. The Skill Confidence Inventory (SCI) measures one's perceived confidence in being able to successfully complete several tasks and activities. It focuses on the vocational domain and is usually combined with the Strong Interest Inventory (SII), which consists of six 10-item General Confidence Themes (GCT) (Betz et al., 1996). Another measurement of self-efficacy is the Generalized Self-Efficacy (GSE) scale, which looks at individuals' adaptation, optimism, and coping in response to adversity. The GSE is typically self-administered as part of a larger questionnaire. It prompts individuals to respond (1) not at all true, (2) hardly true, (3) moderately true, or (4) exactly true to each of the following 10 statements:

1. I can always manage to solve difficult problems if I try hard enough.
2. If someone opposes me, I can find the means and ways to get what I want.
3. It is easy for me to stick to my aims and accomplish my goals.
4. I am confident that I could deal efficiently with unexpected events.

5. Thanks to my resourcefulness, I know how to handle unforeseen situations.
6. I can solve most problems if I invest the necessary effort.
7. I can remain calm when facing difficulties because I can rely on my coping abilities.
8. When I am confronted with a problem, I can usually find several solutions.
9. If I am in trouble, I can usually think of a solution.
10. I can usually handle whatever comes my way.
    (Schwarzer & Jerusalem, 1995)

Pause and Reflect

Pause here to complete the Generalized Self-Efficacy scale and calculate your total score. As with the tools provided in Chapter 1, the intent here is to develop a deeper awareness of your self-efficacy so you can grow it over time (more on this below). It is worth noting that in a study of almost 20,000 individuals completing the GSE in 25 countries, the international average was 29.55—with Japan self-scoring the lowest at 20.22, Costa Rica the highest at 33.19, and the United States falling close to the international average at just above 29 (Scholz et al., 2002).

Our self-efficacy develops over time from four sources, the most influential of which are performance outcomes or mastery experiences. If we experienced success with a task previously, we tend to be more likely to believe in our ability to accomplish the same or a similar task in the future. Chunking large goals into smaller steps enables us to experience mastery and, as a result, remain more committed to goal attainment. According to Bandura (1977), other sources of self-efficacy, in order of influence, include vicarious experiences (comparing our own competence with others' performance), social persuasions (encouragement or discouragement from others about our ability to perform), and physiological feedback (emotional states such as anxiety or stress). More recent research shows that self-efficacy may also develop through a fifth source, visualization. Picturing ourselves achieving a goal has a positive impact on both our self-belief and the likelihood that we will attain the goal (Maddux, 2013).

The Impact of Collective Efficacy

The concept (and impact) of self-efficacy plays out at both the individual and organizational levels in the form of collective efficacy. When a group's confidence increases, so do their results. Sociologists have observed the impact of collective efficacy in response to neighborhood crime (Sampson et al., 1997), workplace productivity (Kim & Shin, 2015), and student performance (Bandura, 1993). Bandura (1977) defines *collective efficacy* as "a group's shared belief in its conjoint capability to organize and execute the courses of action required to produce given levels of attainment" (p. 477). Meta-analysis demonstrates that teachers' beliefs about their schools' abilities are "strongly and positively associated with student achievement across subject areas and in multiple locations" (Eells, 2011, p. 110). In fact, such beliefs show an effect size of 1.57 as a factor influencing student achievement —three times greater than the effect of students' socioeconomic status (Hattie, 2016).

The primary way organizations can increase collective efficacy is by demonstrating *evidence of impact*. We want to know that what we are doing makes a difference—and when it does not, to access a collaborative community to problem solve together. "As an administrator, I follow a model of *listen, learn,* and *lead* to support my staff in building their own collective teacher efficacy," shares Alissa Farias, an elementary school assistant principal. "I know that the more I listen to them, I can learn exactly what they need and then have a better idea of how to lead. Building collective efficacy takes time and patience and is unique to each building. There is no prescribed way to build culture, but through transparency, vulnerability, and unified 'whys,' it can be achieved."

Before examining the many ways we can see evidence of individual and collective impact on our organizations, we need to better understand the conceptual dimensions of the deliberately developmental organizations we aim to be.

Defining Deliberately Developmental Organizations

Harvard developmental psychologists Robert Kegan and Lisa Laskow Lahey, whose work focuses on professional and organizational development, studied three highly successful companies—Bridgewater, Decurion, and NextJump—all of which built cultures focused on people development. "Of course each of these companies tries to hire the most talented people it can, but the moment it does, it seeks to place them in an environment where every job is a kind of tow rope that will pull them in—if they will hold on tightly— into the challenge of developing themselves" (Kegan & Laskow Lahey, 2016, p. 88). The "everyone cultures," as Kegan and Laskow Lahey refer to them, of these deliberately developmental organizations have three distinct dimensions that make up their conceptual structure: developmental communities (home), developmental aspirations (edge), and developmental practices (groove). We delve into the dimensions of home and edge here as we look to establish trustworthy communities focused on continuous growth. In Chapter 5, we consider the third and final dimension, groove, through the lenses of organizational learning and systems thinking.

Establishing Trustworthy Communities

Becoming a deliberately developmental organization with a strong practice of collective efficacy requires a grounding in trust; members of the organization must feel as though they are "home." Trust grows and is reciprocated through a balance of both vulnerability and strength. "The greatest leaders are vulnerable and strong at the same time," writes Saphier (2019). "And they use those qualities to mobilize irresistible collective action" (p. 12). We must simultaneously demonstrate a collective tolerance for discomfort and a collective commitment to growth to establish a trustworthy community. Put another way: Vulnerability × Strength = Trust.

Shared Vulnerability

In Chapter 3, we discussed some of the different ways we can model vulnerability (e.g., embracing the messenger, being vulnerable first and often, developing and sustaining vulnerability loops). We also looked at some structures we might employ to encourage vulnerable practices, such as after-action reviews and solution groups. When establishing trustworthy communities, vulnerability should not only be modeled but also embraced by all members. It is not a solo act, but a shared commitment to being transparent about and learning from our mistakes. "The key variable is whether our vulnerability is well held, whether we continue to feel respected, worthy, and included, even at our worst. (This feeling is at the heart of what we mean by home...)," write Kegan and Laskow Lahey (2016, p. 116).

For shared vulnerability to be actualized, we cannot get caught up in ranks or titles. Everyone must come to the table on an even playing field as a critical friend regardless of position. We also need to ensure everyone has a "crew" (i.e., accountability partners and/or mentors) to support them. Kenny McKee, coauthor of *Compassionate Coaching: How to Help Educators Navigate Barriers to Professional Growth* (2020), shared this with me:

> In my work as an instructional coach, I have found that creating structures for educators to build positive relationships has been the greatest leverage point in developing collective teacher efficacy....My role in this work is not only to manage the logistics of these forms of collaboration, but to help establish safe spaces in which they can happen. Part of this work includes prioritizing norms for these groups and seeking input on improving them regularly. In addition, I sometimes "match" educators who I believe will be successful in relationships of mutual learning when I am developing collaborative groups.

This shared vulnerability forms when everyone within the organization focuses on people development (most intensively, their own) and culture building.

In deliberately developmental organizations, professional learning is not reserved only for new or struggling staff members. At every level of the organization, people engage in activities, experiences, and conversations that accelerate their growth. It is not an additive, but an integrated experience. Candid dialogue and critique, coaching, resource curation, effective facilitation, and reflection drive team interactions and operations. Team members openly share their growth opportunities and work together to fill these gaps.

Pause and Reflect

Pause to reflect on a time when you have struggled to be professionally vulnerable. What weakness(s) did you hide and why? Were you trying to "look good" or stay safe?

Cultivate Your Capacity

Building on the previous reflection, identify vulnerability gaps, often rooted in self-protected fear, within your own professional practice and the organization as a whole. Consider gaps that arise between the following:

- What we do and what we say
- What we feel and what we say
- What we say at the water cooler and what we say in the meeting
- How we assess someone's performance at the time and how we later provide feedback
- What we know about the organization's principles and how we apply them
- What we know to be the organization's deepest purposes and how we actually operate at every level (Kegan & Laskow Lahey, 2016, p. 101)

Cultivate Organizational Capacity

Provide the following sentence stems to your team and ask them to make a list of what they expect of a trusted leader. Review the responses for patterns and employ them to co-create trust-based community norms:

- I trust that you are <u>competent</u> and can keep the wheels turning by...
- I trust that you think I am a <u>worthwhile person</u> because you...
- I trust that you will make it <u>safe</u> for us to make mistakes by...
- I trust that you will be <u>honest</u>, meaning you...
- I trust your integrity, that is, that your <u>motives</u> are for the interest of the children, not your own career advancement because you...
- I trust you will act <u>courageously</u> by...
- I trust that you make <u>legitimate decisions</u> because you...
- I trust that will deliver <u>results</u>...
- I trust you will show me <u>respect</u> by...
- I trust that you will act in a <u>caring and compassionate</u> way by... (Saphier, 2019, pp. 6–7)

Demonstrated Strength

Establishing trustworthy communities requires us to both share vulnerability and demonstrate strength. "'Strong' means leaders have core values and goals that drive all their behavior," writes Saphier (2019). "They are public and persistent about these goals. Quietly or loudly, and usually with compelling data, they continually put the work in front of staff members and raise a sense of urgency" (p. 12). Some of the most effective leaders I have worked with use a framework such as The 4 Disciplines of Execution (4DX) to guide this work. We explored elements of this framework when we looked at individual goal execution in Chapter 2, but the approach also applies to teams.

- *Discipline 1: Focus on the Wildly Important*—"Focus your finest effort on the one or two goals that will make all the difference, instead of giving mediocre effort to dozens of goals. Execution starts with focus" (McChesney et al., 2016, p. 23).
- *Discipline 2: Act on the Lead Measures*—"The second discipline is to apply disproportionate energy to the activities that drive your lead measures. This provides the leverage for achieving the lag measures.... Lead measures are the 'measures' of the activities most connected to achieving the goal" (McChesney et al., 2016, p. 44).
- *Discipline 3: Keep a Compelling Scoreboard*—"The third discipline is to make sure everyone knows the score at all times, so that they can tell

whether or not they are winning. This is the discipline of engagement. Remember, people play differently when they are keeping score" (McChesney et al., 2016, p. 65).

- *Discipline 4: Create a Cadence of Accountability*—"The fourth discipline is to create a cadence of accountability, a frequently recurring cycle of accounting for past performance and planning to move the score forward. Discipline 4 is where execution actually happens.... Disciplines 1, 2, and 3 set up the game; but until you apply Discipline 4, your team isn't *in* the game" (McChesney et al., 2016, p. 77).

Compelling Data. Strong leaders and team members consistently employ compelling data to motivate their colleagues. They share future goals and past progress in equal measure to build both self- and collective efficacy. By establishing a limited number of goals (Discipline 1) and dedicating concentrated energy to the lead measures that will provide the greatest leverage toward those goals (Discipline 2), they provide team clarity and avoid initiative fatigue. Teams experience progress, and in turn build collective efficacy, because they are collaboratively focused on *the thing* rather than *all the things*.

Sense of Urgency. With a communal commitment to shared vulnerability, teams can keep a compelling scoreboard that transparently illuminates the progress made to date as well as work to still be accomplished (Discipline 3). We are less likely to get caught up in and dragged down by situational barriers, such as conversations about student cohorts of unequal performance and contextual (often temporary) teacher challenges (e.g., medical leave, new hires) when we all own the challenge of getting better together. When teams implement well here, they examine longitudinal and growth data (for both students and themselves) as measures in equal weight to achievement data. They step back to look at the full landscape *and* dig into individual data points and trends.

Showing the scoreboard is not enough, though; effective teams act upon it. They make specific commitments to implement lead measures—those with the greatest leverage—and meet regularly to review their progress and refine their approach. This cadence of accountability ensures the work is a collective effort and not a solo endeavor (Discipline 4). Effective teams use protocols, action planning tools, and learning logs to effectively guide their conversations and inform their next steps (more on this in Chapter 5). Leaders and team members who breed a sense of urgency do more than share compelling data; they help us understand that progress toward the goal(s) is critically important and that we cannot accomplish them alone.

Pause and Reflect

Pause to develop one or two wildly important goals that would make a significant difference in your classroom, school, or community. If possible, draft them as SMARTER goals (see Chapter 2).

Cultivate Your Capacity

Collect data that accurately captures your (or your students') current level of performance as it relates to each goal. What is your baseline? Where are you in relation to the end goal? When possible, try to collect quantitative data, though it is possible to engage in this work with qualitative measures as well.

Next, consider the lead measures that will have the most significant impact on your progress. Select one lead measure you will integrate into your practice over the next two weeks. Take notes during this implementation phase to develop a deeper understanding of your strengths, growth opportunities, and obstacles to improvement.

Share your goals, current performance levels, and selected lead measures with your accountability partner. Request that they check in with you periodically over the two weeks to monitor your progress. At the end of the two weeks, collect an updated data set and meet with your accountability partner to review your next steps.

Cultivate Organizational Capacity

Follow the same steps as those outlined in the preceding section, but implement them for a grade level, grade band, or content area rather than a single classroom and meet in teams instead of pairs. As much as possible, team members should act upon the same lead measures rather than pilot individual strategies. This approach not only supports fidelity of implementation but will also help you collectively identify the most effective approaches.

Promoting Continuous Growth

We have looked at what it means to establish a developmental community grounded in trust—one that makes individuals feel as though they are "home." Now we will turn to the "edge"—our developmental aspirations, not just as individuals but as a collective whole. To step beyond our personal limitations and contribute to becoming a deliberately developmental organization, we need to commit to both a growth mindset and a unifying focus.

Growth Mindset

Carol Dweck, a leading researcher in the fields of personality and social and developmental psychology at Stanford University, introduced the concept of "fixed" and "growth" mindsets in her landmark 2006 book *Mindset: The New Psychology of Success*. According to Dweck's research, which began in the early 1970s, individuals with a fixed mindset "believe that your qualities are carved in stone" (p. 6); that "you can learn new things, but you can't really change how intelligent you are" (p. 12). In contrast, those with a growth mindset believe "that your basic qualities are things you cultivate through your efforts. Although people may differ in every which way—in their initial talents and aptitudes, interests, or temperaments—everyone can change and grow through application and experience" (p. 7). While the concept of a growth mindset has taken hold within schools over the past 15 years, we have not seen it integrated with the same concentration in adult learning spaces. We dialogue with teachers about setting student growth objectives, but the conversations do not often address adult growth.

Adults Can Grow. Developing a growth mindset is a systemic cultural practice. Those who are oriented toward a growth mindset don't just do the necessary work; they do the work a little bit better every day. We need to ask ourselves, "How central are developmental aspirations to the work we do here? Are we deeply committed to growing together and openly modeling growth for one another and our students?" A deliberately developmental organization "enables people to uncover and value their growing edge, and experience themselves as still valuable even as they are screwing up—and they can potentially be even more valuable if they can overcome the limitations they are exposing," write Kegan and Laskow Lahey (2016). "People's limitations are seen as their growing edge—a company resource, an asset—that should be continuously and publicly engaged" (p. 106). In deliberately developmental organizations, adults believe they can grow and support one another's growth and, as a result, experience both personal evolution and professional flourishing.

As we look at adult growth over time, we typically see three plateaus of adult mental complexity: the *socialized* mind, the *self-authoring* mind, and the *self-transforming* mind (all positioned on an axis of mental complexity and time or age). These qualitative levels represent a different way of knowing the world, and we tend to remain on each plateau for a considerable time. The plateaus can help us understand differences in the ways individuals within our organization might view and respond to growth-oriented feedback and actions.

The socialized mind
- We are shaped by the definitions and expectations of our personal environment.
- Our self coheres by its alignment with, and loyalty to, that with which it identifies.
- This sense of self can express itself primarily in our relationships with people, with schools of thought (our ideas and beliefs), or both.

The self-authoring mind

- We are able to step back enough from the social environment to generate an internal seat of judgment, or personal authority, that evaluates and makes choices about external expectations.
- Our self coheres by its alignment with its own belief system, ideology, or personal code; by its ability to self-direct, take stands, set limits, and create and regulate its boundaries on behalf of its own voice.

The self-transforming mind

- We can step back from and reflect on the limits of our own ideology or personal authority; see that any one system or self-organization is in some way partial or incomplete; be friendlier toward contradiction and opposites; seek to hold on to multiple systems rather than project all except one onto the other.
- Our self coheres through its ability not to confuse internal consistency with wholeness or completeness, and through its alignment with the dialectic rather than either pole. (Kegan & Laskow Lahey, 2016, p. 63)

These plateaus and how we are positioned on them significantly affect information flow and our ability to support one another's growth. Without careful tending, a self-authoring mind with a well-tuned filter for focus could (unintentionally) shut out perspectives and ideas from a socialized mind. However, if we are serious about student growth, we must also commit to adult growth across all plateaus. According to Helsing, "if schools are going to be places where students consistently push against the edge of what they don't know, testing new theories, and trying things out while learning from mistakes, those same qualities must be present for their teachers. It's difficult for a teacher to facilitate that type of learning environment if they haven't experienced it themselves" (quoted in Schwartz, 2020, para. 3). As educators, we must model not only content and skills but also the process of learning.

Pause and Reflect

Pause here to self-identify your current plateau of adult mental complexity (i.e., socialized, self-authoring, or self-transforming). There is no "wrong" plateau, and being aware of your position can help you better understand how to respond to the world and others, particularly those who may be on a different level.

Pause and Reflect

Reflect on the ways your team or school supports the development of a growth mindset by responding to the prompts in Figure 4.2.

FIGURE 4.2

Collective Efficacy Reflection: Growth Mindset

Prompt for Reflection	Yes	No	Observations and Considerations
Does your organization help you identify a personal challenge—meaningful to you and valuable for the company— that you can work on in order to grow?			
Are there others who are aware of this growing edge and who care that you transcend it?			
Are you given support to overcome your limitations? Can you name or describe this support?			
Do you experience yourself actively working on transcending this growing edge daily or at least weekly?			
When you do become a more capable version of yourself, is it recognized, is it celebrated, and—when you're ready— are you given the opportunity to keep growing?			

Prompts for reflection come from R. Kegan & L. Laskow Lahey, 2016, *An everyone culture: Becoming a deliberately developmental organization* (pp. 87–88), Harvard Business School Publishing.

See Weakness as Opportunity. Deliberately developmental organizations focused on continuous growth see weakness as an opportunity rather than a deficit. These districts, schools, and teams recognize the vast complexities of the teaching profession and understand that individual educators cannot demonstrate proficiency in all domains simultaneously. They collectively work toward high-expertise teaching by consistently engaging in ongoing content and error analysis to improve their practice.

In this way, teams exhibit a growth mindset at both the individual and group levels. They do not hide poor performance or mistakes, but instead use collaborative time to surface challenges and errors and troubleshoot them together. Phil Echols, a senior organizational and diversity specialist, shared with me the importance of learning from mistakes even as adults:

> The ability to build and maintain relationships is essential to sustainable work. Having high expectations and achieving audacious goals begins with a strong relational foundation. For me, it begins with the ability to model vulnerability, grace, and trust. Learning together and growing together starts with building a culture that celebrates success and learns from mistakes. As adults, we learn from processing our experiences, and individuals and teams must normalize processing time, be it during meetings or between events.

Deliberately developmental teams collect and share data formally and informally to drive their practice. Evidence of strong performance builds collective efficacy, and identified gaps provide opportunities for growth rather than demonstrate failure. Collective efficacy "isn't just growth mindset; it's not just 'rah rah' thinking; it's not just 'Oh we can make a difference!' but it is that combined belief that it is us that causes learning," highlights Hattie (2018). "Because when you fundamentally believe you can make the difference, and then you feed it with the evidence that you are, then that [is what makes it] dramatically powerful." Collective efficacy is more than a team's demonstrated belief that they can grow; it is evidence, over time, that they actually *have* grown. However, collective efficacy is only possible when team members transparently share their progress, or lack thereof, and leverage weaknesses as opportunities for growth.

Companies that do this well have a central location in place to capture errors, lessons learned, and subsequent actions taken. Schools committed to becoming deliberately developmental organizations employ data-analysis tools and learning logs not only as protocols or accountability measures, but also as mechanisms to collect evidence. These resources provide a snapshot of current performance to enable teams to show progress over time. Teams share evidence during meetings and dedicate times to process it together.

Pause and Reflect

Identify a current weakness in your professional practice. Consider how you might reframe it as a growth opportunity. What resources or people might support your growth?

Cultivate Your Capacity

Make a commitment to improve an area of your professional practice. If possible, select an area you may have avoided in the past out of fear or an anticipated high level of challenge.

1. Complete the following statement: "I am committed to getting better at _____." Focus on consistent improvement over time. Frame your commitment in an affirming or positive way.

2. Be brutally honest with yourself. Identify all the actions working against your commitment as well as inactions that may impact your growth. This list will be downright ugly—a collection of things that derail, sabotage, and undermine your improvement. Focus on specific behaviors here rather than feelings or states of mind.

3. Name your fears and concerns. What is the root of your anxiety and self-protection? If you were to engage in actions opposite those you identified in question 2, what feelings surface for you? What are the hidden competing commitments you seek to protect?

4. As you look over your responses to the questions above, consider which core values or big assumptions serve you well and which ones

you might "break" in the interest of growth. How might you leverage your weaknesses as opportunities?

Cultivate Organizational Capacity

Evaluate your teams' current use of meeting time. Are there opportunities to integrate protocols or learning logs to drive more transparent, solutions-oriented conversations grounded in evidence? How might you support your team in demonstrating progress over time to foster a growth mindset as well as build collective efficacy?

Unifying Focus

Deliberately developmental organizations exhibit a growth mindset at both the individual and collective levels and ground themselves in a unifying focus. Growth is intentional and consistent as well as purpose-driven. Not only are members persistently progressing, but they are doing so in the same concentrated direction. In these districts and schools, mission statements represent more than a wall plaque; they call team members to action.

Run on Developmental Principles. A unifying focus requires organizations to ask, "By what set of shared principles do you carry out your mission?" Beyond school vision and values, what objective criteria drive performance and contribute to a common language of practice? Wiggins and McTighe (2007) highlight the importance of learning principles as a part of school design. Learning principles, they write, "safeguard the mission by providing a self-assessment mechanism for ensuring that our practices are valid in terms of what is known and how people learn.... Otherwise, all we have is goodwill and personal beliefs.... If all we have is a mission statement, we have no way to address the endless practical problems and disagreements about teaching that will crop up" (p. 115).

High-reliability organizations (e.g., combat units, surgical teams) face the possibility of mortal danger and run on survival principles (Weick,

1995). They distinguish themselves by detecting weak warning signs and taking strong decisive action. In contrast, developmental organizations, such as schools, focus on emergence and new capabilities. They embrace the possibility of growth and run on developmental principles. Here are two examples of such principles:

- "Engaged and sustained learning, a prerequisite for understanding, requires that learners constantly see the value of their work and feel a growing sense of efficacy when facing worthy challenges" (Wiggins & McTighe, 2007, p. 113).
- "The capacity to deeply understand depends greatly on the capacity to think things anew (and other related habits of mind), because any insight typically requires a safe and supportive environment for questioning assumptions and habits" (Wiggins & McTighe, 2007, p. 114).

Principles provide a unifying focus on a school's mission in action; in essence, mission-critical tasks center a team's work. Look closely at schools and teams to identify those driven by accountability versus those driven by development. The principles that guide their work and the subsequent informal mechanisms that derive from such principles look and sound quite different and produce very different results in terms of learning culture.

Leverage Informal Mechanisms. When deliberately developmental organizations are run firmly according to growth-oriented principles, a set of informal mechanisms begins to emerge and can be leveraged to accelerate collective growth. Common behaviors, norms, and practices surface to further sharpen the organization's unifying focus and, in turn, strengthen its sense of collective efficacy. Leaders and team members can leverage these informal mechanisms to enhance their organization's learning culture through a series of intentional moves (Saphier, 2019):

1. Say it: Be explicit that you value and want to strengthen the norm.
2. Model it: Be a consistent living practitioner of the norm.
3. Organize for it: Create events, forums, and structures that embed learning about the norm.
4. Protect it: Shield those who practice the norm from criticism and consequences.

5. Reward it: Recognize those who act on and commit to the norm.

A unifying focus requires more than stating and modeling expected behaviors; we need to also provide the structures and supports necessary for those behaviors to be actualized and integrated sustainably. If a school values personalized professional learning, it is not enough to talk about it. The school must also provide the system, offerings, and capacity building necessary to normalize a new paradigm in training and development.

The Bottom Line Is All One Thing. Districts and schools offer more flavors than an ice cream shop. The phrase "flavor of the month" in relation to initiative fatigue has become so pervasive within school environments that it is no longer a joke, but rather a cause of sheer exhaustion. And quite honestly, this "shiny ball syndrome" inhibits growth across our learning organizations for both adults and students. The target, or unifying focus, constantly shifts, making it difficult for educators to home in on the school's developmental principles and identify the subsequent norms and actions that constitute "success." Instead, we bounce from strategy to strategy in a never-ending game of Frogger.

Deliberately developmental organizations stop initiative hopping and focus on a single bottom line: We all need to get better. This consistent and laser-focused commitment to growth—at all levels of the organization— provides a safe space to share vulnerability, demonstrate strength, and exhibit a growth mindset. There is both social trust *and* continuous growth.

Pause and Reflect

Reflect on the unifying focus, or lack thereof, driving your district, school, or team. What are the principles pushing your collective work? Do they promote high reliability, accountability, development, or another core value? To what degree do the organization's mission and principles align or misalign?

Cultivate Your Capacity

Work with your team to draft principles that drive your shared work. Ensure they reflect your team's values and accelerate progress toward your goals. Use these principles as guideposts to facilitate team conversations and provide feedback that is not personal but, rather, purpose-driven.

Cultivate Organizational Capacity

Revisit your district's or school's vision and mission. Have principles been established to guide organizational strategy toward these overarching goals? Are the actions educators take each day, including your own, aligned or misaligned with the vision? How might you leverage developmental principles (as well as more informal mechanisms such as behaviors, norms, and practices) to move the needle closer to achieving your school's mission?

More Than the Sum of Its Parts

Building our social-emotional capacity requires tending to self-efficacy as well as collective efficacy. We must develop both self-management and relationship skills, and as adults and educators specifically, we must also commit to action. We must believe in our capacity to grow and evolve (growth mindset), take clear and intentional steps forward (unifying focus), and gather evidence to demonstrate our progress and strengthen our confidence over time (collective efficacy). In these ways, our schools become more than the sum of individual team members; they flourish into deliberately developmental organizations. "There are striking examples where the intelligence of the team exceeds the intelligence of the individuals of the team, and where teams develop extraordinary capacities for coordinated action," writes Senge (2006). "When teams are truly learning, not only are they producing extraordinary results, but the individual members are growing more rapidly than could have occurred otherwise" (p. 9). Schools move from a community of social trust to one of social cohesion.

Fostering the discipline of collective efficacy requires that we look not only to the processes by which our schools are run but also to the people—at all levels—who run them. Deliberately developmental organizations focus on people development more than process refinement. They invest in professional capital over business capital (Hargreaves & Fullan, 2012). "It is one thing to be relentless about continuously improving the processes by which work gets done; it is quite another to be relentless about continuously improving the people who do the work," write Kegan and Laskow Lahey (2016, pp. 102–103). In this way, our role as leaders and team members focuses on facilitative growth rather than directed accountability.

School director and ASCD faculty member Jason Flom shared with me:

> When we started our school, we didn't know the term *collective efficacy*. However, in hindsight, it is clear we had at least part of it right—confidence in our capacity to effect change collaboratively. Blind confidence? Maybe. But we trusted each other and our shared commitment to our vision and mission.... Over 20 years later, the evidence is all around. Yes, in the data of our neurodiverse community, but in more important ways as well. Our faculty return year after year. There's laughter in our buildings, at staff meetings, and around the proverbial water cooler. There's not only a sense of what we can do, for us founding faculty who are still here, there's a sense of what we have done, and continue to do, together.

Collective efficacy creates spaces where adults evolve personally and flourish professionally.

Pause and Reflect

The integration guide in Appendix D (p. 181) brings these concepts together to guide your growth in the discipline of collective efficacy, developing not only as an individual but also as an organization. Pause here to review the integration guide and identify the next steps you will take to build your capacity in this area.

The capacity-building plan in Appendix D (p. 182) captures all the action steps for reflection, cultivating your capacity, and cultivating organizational capacity outlined in this chapter.

Extend the Learning Loop

The resources outlined in Figure 4.3 may provide additional support as you continue developing the discipline of collective efficacy. Additional space has been included for you to capture your own resources for exploration as you develop a capacity-building plan for yourself and your team(s).

In Chapter 5, we explore the specific practices of learning organizations and the systems that propel their growth, examining the ecology they embody to build capacity at all levels. "Most organizations have mission statements," write Kegan and Laskow Lahey (2016). "They have purposes. They have goals. They have procedures. They have employee manuals. They may also have mottos or mantras that reflect principles—'the client comes first'; 'something only we can do'; 'progress is our most important product.' But without a pervasive ecology—structures, practices, tools, and shared language that allow the organization to embody and orient to these values— they become slogans rather than drivers of the culture" (p. 108). In the pages that follow, we will look at systems not just as things but as interdependent relationships that promote social-emotional, professional, and organizational growth.

FIGURE 4.3

Recommended Resources: Collective Efficacy

☐ "Collective Teacher Efficacy (CTE) According to John Hattie" (https://visible-learning.org/2018/03/collective-teacher-efficacy-hattie)

☐ *Collective Efficacy: How Educators' Beliefs Impact Student Learning* by Jenni Donohoo (Corwin, 2016)

☐ *Leading Collective Efficacy: Powerful Stories of Achievement and Equity* by Stefani Arzonetti Hite and Jenni Donohoo (Corwin, 2020)

☐ "The Power of Collective Efficacy," in *Educational Leadership,* by Jenni Donohoo, John Hattie, and Rachel Eells (2018) (www.ascd.org/el/articles/the-power-of-collective-efficacy)

☐ *An Everyone Culture: Becoming a Deliberately Developmental Organization* by Robert Kegan and Lisa Laskow Lahey, with Andy Fleming, Deborah Helsing, and Matthew Miller (Harvard Business Review Press, 2016)

☐ "The Key to Adaptable Companies Is Relentlessly Developing People," in *Harvard Business Review,* by Andy Fleming (2016) (https://hbr.org/2016/10/the-key-to-adaptable-companies-is-relentlessly-developing-people)

☐ "Why Focusing on Adult Learning Builds a School Culture Where Students Thrive," in *MindShift,* by Katrina Schwartz (2020) (www.kqed.org/mindshift/54750/why-focusing-on-adult-learning-builds-a-school-culture-where-students-thrive)

☐ *The 4 Disciplines of Execution: Achieving Your Wildly Important Goals* by Chris McChesney, Sean Covey, and Jim Huling, with Beverly Walker and Scott Thele (Simon & Schuster, 2022)

☐ *Mindset: The New Psychology of Success* by Carol Dweck (Ballantine, 2007)

☐ *Schooling by Design: Mission, Action, and Achievement* by Grant Wiggins and Jay McTighe (ASCD, 2007) (Note that sample learning principles are included on pp. 113–114.)

☐ "Sense and Reliability," in *Harvard Business Review,* by Diane Coutu (2003) (https://hbr.org/2003/04/sense-and-reliability)

☐

☐

☐

☐

5

ORGANIZATIONAL LEARNING

At the heart of a learning organization is
a shift of mind—from seeing ourselves as
separate from the world to connected to the world,
from seeing problems as caused by someone or
something "out there" to seeing how our own actions
create the problems we experience. A learning
organization is a place where people are continually
discovering how they create their reality.

—Peter Senge

Getting into the Groove

organizational (adjective): the act or process of organizing; the state or manner of being organized

learning (noun): the act or process of acquiring knowledge or skill; modification of behavior through practice, training, or experience

Educator capacity building includes attuning and aligning ourselves as well as gaining perspective from and strengthening the collective efficacy of our teams. It is about knowing ourselves and about understanding and responding in growth-promoting ways toward others. In this final chapter, we explore the discipline of organizational learning. We will look at the core competencies that propel learning beyond our self and our teams—an ecology of interdependent relationships that sustains a *culture* of growth parallel to *individuals* and *teams* who grow.

In Chapter 4, we examined the conceptual structures of developmental communities ("home") and developmental aspirations ("edge"). As Kegan and Laskow Lahey (2016) note, deliberately developmental organizations "live out their developmental principles through an immersive and seamless set of practices, which we call its groove" (p. 113). This "groove" includes regular practices and routines that define "how we do business" in our districts, schools, and teams. Any educator who has transitioned from district to district or school to school recognizes and feels these practical differences within each school environment—often from the very first day. When I worked as an administrator in a K–12 school, I even noticed differences within the same building between grade bands and curricular areas. These differences surface in behaviors as mundane as unspoken photocopier norms and as noteworthy as the cadence and tone of staff meetings and significant celebrations. Developmental communities lay the foundation and developmental principles set the standard, but it is our regular practices and routines (or systems) that engineer them.

Practices and Systems

In Chapter 2, we delved into the importance of goal-aligned habits and rituals for individuals. The same holds true at the organizational level. "These [organizational] practices include how meetings are structured, how employee performance is monitored and discussed, and how people talk to one another about their work and the challenges they face personally and in advancing the interests of the company," write Kegan and Laskow Lahey (2016, pp. 113–114). Informal mechanisms such as behaviors and norms help reinforce developmental principles, but consistent systemic practices are what sustain and strengthen them.

When I partner with schools to design and facilitate more personalized professional learning models, the tension between structure and agency inevitably emerges within almost every school community. Leaders want to empower staff members with agency in their professional learning opportunities and implementation, but they also affirm the need for systemic accountability. The more I have engaged in this work, the more I have come to realize the two are not mutually exclusive. In fact, in many ways, clear and consistent structures promote efficiency and provide teachers with space (i.e., time and cognitive capacity) to take a more learner-directed approach. When learning experiences are too open-ended and unstructured, teachers experience confusion and frustration. I mention this because the terms *practice* and *system* have come to assume a negative connotation in many educational settings. We get stuck in the nuances of "best practices" and "systemic reform." We see these concepts as synonymous with limited autonomy and strict accountability measures.

However, it is not the notion of common practices and systems that is problematic as much as it is the types of systems we continue to employ. "Schools are not 'broken' and in need of fixing," write Senge and colleagues (2000). "They are a social institution under stress that needs to evolve" (p. 52). Our practices and systems have not kept pace and evolved with our developmental communities and aspirations. In many ways, they are still reflective of factory-based rather than growth-oriented models of learning. When faced with technical problems, adaptive challenges, and generative opportunities, we need schools equipped with the core competencies of learning organizations, prepared to purposely focus and filter these events through the most appropriate people and processes. As my colleagues and I noted (Rodman et al., 2020), "Fully committing to social emotional learning for both students and educators requires that we revisit the (often woefully outdated) structural systems that define the environments we have come to classify as schools... and re-examine how we conceive of time, space, and connection within education" (p. 58).

We must build our professional and organizational capacity on an individual, team, *and* systems level. Figure 5.1 provides an organizational learning blueprint to guide your exploration of this discipline.

As you read this chapter, you can use the QR code or visit https://www
.thelearningloop.com/book-organizational-learning to access editable
PDF versions of the reflection and planning tools included throughout
the text. Use the case-sensitive password "StillLearning" to download
the resources.

FIGURE 5.1

Capacity-Building Blueprint: Organizational Learning

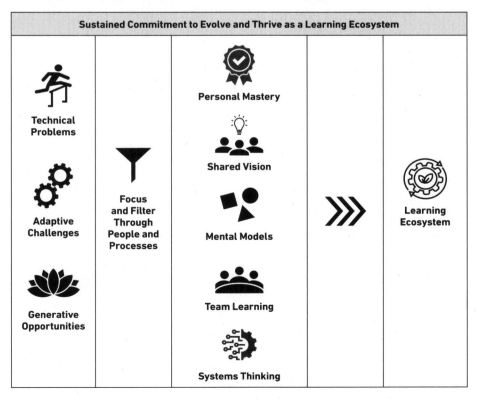

Technical, Adaptive, and Generative Events

As we engage in the work of organizational learning and develop systems that promote sustainability, it is critical that we distinguish among technical, adaptive, and generative events. Over time, the purpose of schools and their respective responsibilities have evolved, but the systems that undergird them have not. Many if not most school systems are grounded in efficiency and consistency rather than inquiry and ideation. For the most part, our schools still react in a technical manner even when faced with adaptive challenges (e.g., COVID-19) or generative opportunities (e.g., the post-pandemic return to in-person schooling). Recognizing the distinctions among technical problems, adaptive challenges, and generative opportunities can ensure schools appropriately define the circumstance, engage the right stakeholders, focus the work, and implement with effectiveness. The following two lists, adapted by the University of Chicago's Network for College Success (n.d.) from the work of Heifetz and colleagues (Heifetz et al., 2009; Heifetz & Laurie, 1997), outline the distinctions between the first two types of problems:

Technical problems

1. Easy to identify
2. Often lend themselves to quick and easy (cut-and-dried) solutions
3. Often can be solved by an authority or expert
4. Require change in just one or a few places; often contained within organizational boundaries
5. People are generally receptive to technical solutions
6. Solutions can often be implemented quickly—even by edict

Adaptive challenges

1. Difficult to identify (easy to deny)
2. Require changes in values, beliefs, roles, relationships, and approaches to work
3. People with the problem do the work of solving it
4. Require change in numerous places; usually across organizational boundaries
5. People often resist even acknowledging adaptive challenges.

6. "Solutions" require experiments and new discoveries; they can take a long time to implement and cannot be implemented by edict. (Network for College Success, n.d., p. 19)

Generative opportunities (Carroll et al., 2002) are characterized as follows:

1. Require proactive information seeking
2. Require innovations in values, beliefs, roles, relationships, and approaches to work
3. People embrace opportunities with the guidance of an authority or expert.
4. Require a change in numerous places; usually across organizational boundaries, work structures, and even roles
5. People resist—and often fight against—generative opportunities due to the required shift in practice.
6. Leveraging "opportunities" requires question generation, ideation, and design thinking across a diverse range of stakeholders.

All three types of events continue to flow into schools, but circumstances are becoming more and more adaptive. Similarly, generative opportunities to reimagine innovative constructs of schooling and professional learning are presenting themselves in ways not previously seen. One of the most common mistakes across organizations is trying to meet adaptive challenges through technical means; there is a difference, after all, between response and reaction (Heifetz et al., 2009) as well as creation (Senge, 2006). In this sense, schools must take steps to react, respond, *and* create.

Core Competencies of Learning Organizations

In the sections that follow, we will examine the core competencies of learning organizations: personal mastery, shared vision, mental models, team learning, and systems thinking (Senge, 2006). Taken together, these competencies enable organizations to aspire, work collaboratively, and cope with complexity regardless of whether events are technical, adaptive, or generative. The competencies promote learning organizations driven by development rather than production, focusing on growth over efficiency. Within each competency, we will examine ideas for moving from concept to systemic practice.

Personal Mastery

Personal mastery is the creative tension between our personal vision (what we want) and current reality (where we are relative to what we want). The competency is best visualized as the polar ends of a stretched rubber band. Organizational learning is not possible without personal mastery, and for many schools, this core competency is missing or underrealized. Schools that enable and elevate personal mastery essentially bring the intrapersonal disciplines of attunement and alignment to a systems level. "Organizations learn only through individuals who learn," writes Senge (2006). "Individual learning does not guarantee organizational learning. But without it no organizational learning occurs" (p. 129). The challenge with school systems is that they can be too stable at times, and their structures do not always promote growth. Opportunities for formal positional shifts are limited. As a result, educators lack a feeling of forward movement and progress. They feel stuck, seek external networks for validation and social promotion, and burn out.

Tending to personal mastery at a systems level requires that schools practice constructive destabilization. They need to create more formal growth opportunities within positions—to engage in professional learning with the U.S. Department of Education's Teach to Lead program or the Center for Teaching Quality, establish more robust teacher leadership positions, build capacity for peer-to-peer professional learning facilitation, attend conferences, facilitate coaching conversations, draft progression and transition plans, and so on. In addition to horizontal progressions (e.g., teacher leader to administrator) and professional network and skill development, schools can also reframe the notion of "position fit" to promote growth rather than comfortability. For example, shifting staff members laterally between grade levels or departments continues to develop their practice and strengthen teams, provided these individuals have colleagues who will support them through the transition. Finally, schools must not back down from the complexity of the profession. In Chapter 4, we noted the robust intricacies of the teaching role. The work is challenging, but it should not be diluted out of fear of burnout. Instead, challenges should be welcomed and navigated as a collective community.

Pause and Reflect

Pause here to reflect on your own personal mastery within your current position. Are you experiencing creative tension between your personal vision and your current reality? Does your school practice constructive destabilization to promote growth?

Cultivate Your Capacity

Increase or induce more consistent creative tension between your personal vision and your current reality. Look for constructive destabilization opportunities and share them with your team or accountability partner as possible levers for growth.

Cultivate Organizational Capacity

Reflect on the degree to which intrapersonal attunement and alignment disciplines are positioned as solo development opportunities versus directly integrated into your school's professional learning model. For example, are growth profiles included as a part of your educator growth model or team norm-setting processes? Do educators have an opportunity to engage in professional learning opportunities focused on effective goal setting and action plan implementation? Are clear organizational norms established around calendar use and communication efficiency? Or are these capacity-building areas exclusively learner-driven rather than organization-led? How might your school or district practice constructive destabilization through formal positions, learning opportunities, and staffing shifts? Beyond educator evaluations, what opportunities exist for individuals to experience personal mastery and continuous growth?

Shared Vision

Many years ago, when I was preparing for my educational leadership Praxis exam, there was a running joke among our principal cohort about how to respond to a question if we were unsure about the most appropriate leadership or management approach. After a few of us completed the test, the consensus on the best response was undeniable: When in doubt, form a committee. I look back on this now and can only smile. It seemed so simple, so contrived—almost too easy. Yet, after having engaged in mission and vision work now as an administrator, a board leader, and a consultant, I realize how much we overlook or dilute this step in the process. We may administer surveys, host focus groups, and even hire consultants to facilitate cross-sectional stakeholder conversations and analyze participants' responses for patterns, but in this work, one group's voice never quite comes through loudly enough: that of the educators engaged in the deep, day-to-day work within our learning organizations. In fact, research suggests that only 8.5 percent of teachers strongly agree that faculty and leaders share a vision, yet fostering a shared vision is one of the top three elements of instructional leadership most associated with student achievement (Ingersoll et al., 2017).

Visioning efforts demand looking ahead, but they also require embracing the energy and garnering the commitment of team members here and now. Shared visions—at least the ones we passionately pursue with collective vitality—do not emerge solely from survey responses, sticky notes, and chart paper; rather, they reflect team members' own personal visions. "A shared vision is not an idea," writes Senge (2006). "It is, rather, a force in people's hearts, a force of impressive power.... Few, if any forces in human affairs are as powerful as shared vision" (p. 92). In its truest sense at the organizational level, a shared vision is a systemic manifestation of the alignment between purpose and practice. It reflects an understanding of who we are, both individually and collectively, and a commitment to who we seek to be, for both ourselves and as model learners for our students.

Shared vision represents more than a hallway plaque in a school's entryway or a tagline on the district website. At its core, shared vision is an active expression of goal orientation and actualization at a systems level. "Shared vision is vital for the learning organization because it provides the focus and energy for learning," notes Senge (2006). "While adaptive learning is possible without vision, generative learning occurs only when people are striving to accomplish something that matters deeply to them. In fact, the whole idea of generative learning—expanding your ability to create—will seem abstract and meaningless *until* people become excited about a vision they truly want to accomplish" (p. 192). This distinction offers context for why so many schools responded effectively to the adaptive challenges of COVID-19 but have failed to harness the generative opportunities in teaching and learning (at all levels) that continue to present themselves.

It is not uncommon for schools and organizations to engage in visioning processes with varying levels of buy-in. Senge (2006) outlines a continuum of attitudes toward a vision, including commitment, enrollment, genuine compliance, formal compliance, grudging compliance, noncompliance, and apathy. Leaders often mistake compliance for enrollment or commitment because compliance exists at so many levels and has been a driving force within organizations for decades. Schools that lean into the core competency of shared vision conceive of ways to bring it to life beyond school improvement plans and district letterhead. Shared vision surfaces as a student-written pledge, community-building activities, or student and staff member recognition at awards assemblies. It guides team protocols for evaluating assessment quality, specifically how assessments are aligned to vision-driven benchmarks and grade-level progressions that have been outlined for students. A shared vision is incorporated into hiring and performance materials such as job descriptions, interview rubrics, and observation tools. It filters curricular program adoption processes and focuses budget planning. Shared vision is both "what we say we do" *and* "what we actually do"—even when others are not looking.

Pause and Reflect

Pause here to assess the degree to which your district's or school's vision is truly shared as a reflection of its members' personal visions. Are educators' voices heard in equal weight as compared with other stakeholder groups?

Cultivate Your Capacity

Identify elements of your district or school's vision that, from your perspective, reflect collective members' personal visions. Which components inspire action and which ones feel generalized, sound like stock language, and/or lack clarity and commitment? For example, some vision statements include subjective descriptors such as "world-class," "high-quality," and "excellence," which lack clarity and specificity. In contrast, others use phrases like "cultivate independent, adaptive problem solvers" or "model and practice meaningful collaboration and consensus building" that act as community calls to action. Share your reflections with your accountability partner or team and solicit their feedback. Then, incorporate their feedback into your vision summary and present it to your supervisor for further consideration.

Cultivate Organizational Capacity

Over time, the purpose of schooling has significantly evolved, and it continues to shift and change. However, through these evolutions, we can generally summarize the long-term goals of "school" (at least within the current context) into the following categories:

- Academic excellence and intellectual preparation for higher education
- The development of mature habits of mind and attitudes
- Artistic and aesthetic sensibility and sensitivity
- Health, wellness, and athletic development
- Character—mature social, civic, and ethical conduct
- Personal skill development and professional direction (Wiggins & McTighe, 2007, p. 11)

The shared vision established and executed within each learning organization will generally lead back to one or more of these categories, but its energy is gathered through collective commitment, not compliance.

To what degree does your district or school vision and mission reflect members' strengths and aspirations? Does your shared vision actively drive organizational systems and day-to-day operations, and if not, why not? Does your vision need to be rewritten, revised, or reinvigorated? "Without a *commitment* to mission," write Wiggins and McTighe (2007), "we don't really have a school; we just have a home for freelance tutors of subjects" (p. 25). Is your organization's vision blueprint clear enough for others to act on it? Reflect on the degree to which the collective values of your school's mission and vision are evident in its learning principles, curriculum, assessment, instructional programs and practices, hiring, appraisal, professional learning, policies, structures, governance, and resource allocation. Do your organizational practices directly align to district and/or school goals? If not, what recommendations might you make for further consideration?

Mental Models

In Chapter 3, we explored the concepts of schema and perspective taking as they relate to better understanding others within our learning communities and being open to changes in our own practices—even if these practices have been ingrained for many years. As Senge (2006) notes, mental models—"surfacing, testing, and improving our internal pictures of how the world works" (p. 163)—exist in some form within all organizations; they are not merely an individual construct. Organizations that effectively integrate the competency of mental models leverage infrastructures to move principles to practice. They push the boundaries of "business as usual" and instead ask, "Why not?" According to Senge (2006), the core competency of mental models includes the following elements:

- Facing up to distinctions between espoused theories (what we say) and theories-in-use (the implied theory in what we do)
- Recognizing "leaps of abstraction" (noticing our jumps from observation to generalization)
- Exposing the "left-hand column" (articulating what we normally do not say)
- Balancing inquiry and advocacy (skills for effective collaborative learning) (p. 176)

Surfacing and testing mental models requires organizations to nurture self-awareness and reflective skills and establish a culture that promotes inquiry. "Reflective practice is the essence of the discipline of mental models," writes Senge. "Without reflective and interpersonal learning skills, learning is inevitably reactive, not generative. Generative learning… requires people at all levels who can surface and challenge their mental models before external circumstances compel them to do so" (p. 177). In the same way the discipline of perspective calls on us as individuals to be reflective practitioners, the competency of mental models looks to districts and schools to be reflective learning organizations. Reflective practice, both individual and collective, means reflecting on thinking while acting— learning by doing.

Learning organizations leverage mental models by creating a shared language and reflection tools to guide their practice. In schools that do this effectively, the shared vision permeates all aspects of the learning community. Learning principles, leadership agreements, and team norms emanate from the vision. Performance indicators and growth targets are not merely phrases on an evaluation rubric used one or two times per year, but concepts interwoven into team conversations, co-planning meetings, pre- and post-observation reflections, and debriefs. A shared understanding exists for what these mental models look and sound like in practice, and when confusion does exist, clear examples, videos, and peer observations help bring clarity. The gap between espoused theories and theories-in-use closes because individuals share the mutual language and tools necessary to articulate the "elephant in the room" often left unspoken and balance both inquiry and advocacy.

Schools demonstrating strength with mental models post their norms in their meeting space, review them at each gathering, and draw team members back to them when discussion veers off-course. They take time to clearly define terms such as *curriculum, assessment, program, strategy,* and *practice*—education vernacular that can carry many meanings and be subject to different interpretations. Professional learning focuses on sense making as much as it does strategy implementation. Mental modeling is not synonymous with unanimous agreement, but it is built on shared under-standing and respect. Mental models pave the way for effective dialogue and, ultimately, team learning.

Pause and Reflect

Pause here to identify mental models that surface, test, and improve learn-ing practices within your organization. Are these mental models simply cog-nitive constructs, or are they paired with clearly defined shared language and reflection tools that help to norm their application?

Cultivate Your Capacity

Identify a mental model aligned with your organization's shared vision that could be strengthened by common language, a clearer definition, or a reflec-tion tool. Draft a summary of the model that includes a detailed definition and examples or create an artifact that fills this gap, and share it with your team for their feedback and refinement.

Cultivate Organizational Capacity

Over time, mental models may lose their relevance and usefulness. For example, mental models around technology integration look incredibly different in schools today than they did 20 years ago. From an organizational perspective, retiring outdated mental models is as important as establishing and institutionalizing new ones. Select one mental model that could benefit from refinement as well as one you might seek to discard. In your organizational leadership practices, try to maintain a proportional relationship between new additions and thoughtful eliminations to sustain momentum and reduce initiative fatigue.

Team Learning

Team learning aligns and develops the capacity of individuals to achieve their shared vision. A lack of team learning may be one of the most prevalent causes of educator burnout. Without it, staff meetings drag on, professional learning feels like an act of compliance rather than collaboration, and action plans fill with accountability measures and administrative tasks instead of impact-driven movements. When we look at deliberately developmental organizations that have fully embraced the concept of "groove," we see authentic team learning propelled by immersive and seamless sets of practices. As Senge (2006) writes, "The fundamental characteristic of the relatively unaligned team is wasted energy. Individuals may work extraordinarily hard, but their efforts do not efficiently translate to team effort. By contrast, when a team becomes more aligned, a commonality of direction emerges, and individuals' energies harmonize. There is less wasted energy. In fact, a resonance or synergy develops" (p. 217). These teams are in the groove; much like a jazz ensemble, they play as one. Team learning is essentially a sustained systemization of collective efficacy.

Teams that learn see alignment as a necessary condition for empower-ment rather than a constraint or threat to individual autonomy. According to Senge (2006, p. 219), such teams do the following:

1. Think insightfully about complex issues.
2. Take innovative, coordinated action and develop operational trust to complement one another's actions.
3. Foster and connect to other learning teams.

Developing the competency of team learning requires skillful dialogue and discussion. Much like perspective taking, such dialogue asks individuals to suspend their assumptions or to "hang together" and "hold the context." These practices allow for a freer flow of communication. Teams that learn often feel their time together "flies by." They do not always remember who said or contributed what, but instead appreciate coming to a shared under-standing of the collective work that needs to be done. In this sense, team learning becomes a *flow activity*—it "provides a sense of discovery, a creative feeling of transporting [individuals] into a new reality. It push[es people] to higher levels of performance" (Csikszentmihalyi, 1990, p. 74). However, teams do not achieve flow by chance. A careful intersection between chal-lenge and skill maintains team momentum. Move too fast, and it produces anxiety; too slowly, and boredom ensues. Team learning develops through a commitment to consistent, vision-aligned practice. It requires careful and intentional application of mental models in day-to-day interactions, meetings, and events. "It cannot be stressed too much that team learning is a *team skill*," writes Senge (2006). "Learning teams learn how to learn together" and need "ways to practice together so that they can develop their collective learning skills" (p. 240). Recall that one of the primary sources of collective efficacy is shared mastery experiences; teams need to see the results of their combined efforts.

In Chapter 3, we looked at protocols as a vehicle to facilitate perspective taking. At the organizational level, schools that effectively engineer team learning consistently use those kinds of protocols, but they position them alongside institutionalized tools and structures to ensure regular and con-sistent implementation across teams. For example, curricular departments that engage in effective team learning might facilitate conversations about one another's unit plans with a tuning protocol or review student work with a success analysis protocol to better understand how others approach their instructional planning processes and how their techniques resonate with students. Links to examples of both protocols are included in Figure 5.2 (p. 163). Note that teams who elevate this work to an organizational or systemic level establish a set of tools and processes—beyond just a protocol—to both scaffold and accelerate team learning. They might develop a detailed peer review schedule at the beginning of the year and further maximize teams' collaboration time by having each presenter meet with their department chair or curriculum coordinator to prepare prior to the team meeting. Team members use common note-taking tools to capture insights and guide discussion, and administrators follow up with presenters following each peer review to walk through their action plan and subsequent changes in practice. In this way, the disciplines of perspective and collective efficacy are amplified from an individual and team practice to an organizational one.

Team learning embeds reflective practices so deeply into the fabric of an organization's infrastructure that the discussion and subsequent action plans simply flow. From an adult learning perspective, individuals engage in action reflection learning (ARL), which posits learning as the sum of P + Q + R (Marquardt et al., 2009; Revans, 1983):

(L) Learning =
(P) Programmed Established Knowledge +
(Q) Questioning Insight (including both open- and close-ended action-based questions) +
(R) Reflection

By structuring the collaborative process, we free up members' cognitive capacity to tend to data and dialogue rather than deflection. In fact, research has found such an approach to increase team productivity by over 30 percent (Revans, 1982). "Important aspects of embedded reflective practices include collaborative examination of student learning data, identification of evidence-based approaches, repeated trial of evidence-based strategies in classrooms, and the re-examination of evidence to determine collective impact," write Hite and Donohoo (2021). "Without a structure to help guide teachers through the stages of a professional learning process or cycle, the managerial demands of day-to-day instruction often sidetrack teams" (p. 88). Hite and Donohoo stress the importance of teams selecting the right protocol or structure for their collaborative dynamic and purpose *and* adhering to the stages. In this way, teams avoid activity traps, or what Katz and colleagues (2009) call "a focus on the doings and not the outcomes" (p. 41). Additionally, teams should avoid the temptation to make members more comfortable by revising a protocol or skipping steps. Deliberately developmental organizations, or DDOs, "take a more fundamental approach to keeping collective work on track than merely setting goals and monitoring progress toward them, even if the DDO approach may cause individuals discomfort," note Kegan and colleagues (2016, p. 118). The power of progress lies in the messy uncomfortable spaces, and protocols and action planning tools help us sit in these spaces a bit longer.

It is also worth noting that we naturally turn to protocols to help us process technical problems (e.g., poor attendance data, declining benchmark scores) but are less inclined to use them to respond to adaptive challenges and design generative solutions. My hope is that schools recognize the power of these processes and of action reflection learning to facilitate deeper and more difficult discussions and employ them to develop more creative and innovative solutions.

Pause and Reflect

Identify your organization's team learning strengths. When are they most in the groove? At what points do dialogue and collaboration simply flow? What protocols, preparation processes, note-taking guides, and action planning tools help systematize perspective taking and collective efficacy to achieve organizational-level team learning?

Cultivate Your Capacity

Identify a groove point with the potential to accelerate organizational progress through team learning that suffers from a bit of friction. Consider how
you might reduce resistance through dialogue or discussion tools and implementation guides. Share a draft and pilot it with your team, making note of
improvements through consistent practice.

Cultivate Organizational Capacity

Revisit the concept of teams across your organization. Are they merely
constructs organized by content area, grade level, and position, or do they
hold greater value in terms of organizational development? How might you
reconceive of the notion of teams within your district or school to produce
generative learning opportunities accelerated by flow and guided by structures, protocols, and implementation tools? What does it look like, sound
like, and feel like to experience perspective taking and collective efficacy on
an organizational level, guided by your shared vision and mental models and
fueled by individuals empowered by personal mastery?

Systems Thinking

It is not by chance that *systems thinking* is the fifth and final competency
of learning organizations. It overlays the other competencies and serves as
a connective mesh that binds parts to the whole. Systems thinking enables
organizations to react and respond to complexity, create generative learning
opportunities, and move from blaming to understanding. It "is a discipline
for seeing wholes," writes Senge (2006). "It is a framework for seeing interrelationships rather than things, for seeing patterns of change rather than
static snapshots" (p. 68). Chief academic officer Hannah Gbenro approaches

systems thinking as a sort of biomatrix, believing that people and processes need to be considered in concert with one another rather than as competing entities. For this reason, she maps out teams and their functions side-by-side with components of the district's shared vision to ensure they move in harmony. A system should not be considered a binding structure that inhibits autonomy, but instead a thriving ecosystem that promotes growth.

Schools that operate as flourishing ecosystems have staff members who consistently show up and trust the process. They recognize that small steps amount to big leaps and remain focused even when the work is difficult and tiring. Individuals say "no" as much as (or more than) they say "yes" to remain aligned with their shared vision, mental models, and team learning structures.

Growth-Oriented Ecosystems

It would be (comparatively) easy to sit back and individually soak in the content and strategies of attunement, alignment, and perhaps even perspective, without tending to the disciplines of collective efficacy and organizational learning. However, educator social-emotional capacity building is precisely what the concept denotes—social. It relies on our connections to one another in equal or greater measure to self-development. To engage in this work, we must commit not only to ourselves but also to one another on a team and systems level. "Moving beyond survival to self-care and social-emotional growth requires consistent commitment—not just from leaders but from educators collectively. We need to recognize and affirm that if we are going to show up for students, we need to show up for ourselves [and one another] first" (Rodman et al., 2020, p. 58).

More than 15 years ago, in Senge's seminal work on organizational learning, he outlined a path ahead for schools. He recognized all of us as "systems citizens" and noted that "innovations needed in education represent a bigger task than educators can accomplish in isolation; they will need to be co-created by a microcosm of the whole system, including business and the students themselves" (2006, p. 362). Almost two decades later, in the shadow of a global pandemic, this statement could not ring truer. Educators are not cogs in the wheel of an efficiency-based educational system. We have a collective responsibility to step forward as citizens in a growth-oriented ecosystem. In my conversation with her, Patrice Dawkins-Jackson of the Carnegie Foundation for the Advancement of Teaching spoke in terms of urging us forward: "Move the work ahead. This does not happen by chance; it flourishes from an intention to be transparent, embrace failure as an engine, and create a culture of reciprocal learning." The time to strengthen professional and organizational capacity, sustain growth-oriented practices, and create thriving learning ecosystems is now.

Pause and Reflect

The integration guide in Appendix E (p. 185) brings these concepts together to guide your growth in the discipline of organizational learning as a learning professional. Pause here to review the integration guide and identify the next steps you will take to build your capacity in this area.

The capacity-building plan in Appendix E (p. 186) captures all the action steps for personal mastery, shared vision, mental models, and team learning outlined in this chapter. (Note that specific action steps for systems thinking are not included because all this collective work constitutes systems thinking.)

Extend the Learning Loop

The resources outlined in Figure 5.2 may provide additional support as you continue developing the discipline of organizational learning. Additional space has been included for you to capture your own resources for exploration as you develop a capacity-building plan for yourself and your team(s).

FIGURE 5.2

Recommended Resources: Organizational Learning

☐ *The Fifth Discipline: The Art and Practice of the Learning Organization* by Peter M. Senge (Random House Business, 2006)

☐ *Schools That Learn (Updated and Revised): A Fifth Discipline Fieldbook for Educators, Parents, and Everyone Who Cares About Education* by Peter Senge, Nelda Cambron-McCabe, Timothy Lucas, Bryan Smith, Janis Dutton, and Art Kleiner (Currency, 2012)

☐ *Leadership Without Easy Answers* by Ronald Heifetz (Belknap, 1998)

☐ "A Survival Guide for Leaders," in *Harvard Business Review,* by Ronald Heifetz and Marty Linsky (2002) (https://hbr.org/2002/06/a-survival-guide-for-leaders)

☐ *The Practice of Adaptive Leadership: Tools and Tactics for Changing Your Organization and the World* by Ronald Heifetz, Alexander Grashow, and Marty Linsky (Harvard Business Press, 2009)

☐ *Schooling by Design: Mission, Action, and Achievement* by Grant Wiggins and Jay McTighe (ASCD, 2007)

☐ "Eight Things Teams Do to Sabotage Their Work," in *Educational Leadership,* by Allison Rodman and Jill Thompson (2019) (www.ascd.org/el/articles/eight-things-teams-do-to-sabotage-their-work)

☐ *Protocols for Professional Learning* by Lois Brown Easton (ASCD, 2009)

☐ *Facilitating Teacher Teams and Authentic PLCs: The Human Side of Leading People, Protocols, and Practices* by Daniel R. Venables (ASCD, 2018)

☐ "The Tuning Protocol: A Framework for Personalized Professional Development," in *Edutopia,* by Jess Hughes (2016) (www.edutopia.org/blog/tuning-protocol-framework-personalized -professional-development-jess-hughes)

☐ Tuning Protocol Examples from the School Reform Initiative:

   • www.schoolreforminitiative.org/download/tuning-protocol

   • www.schoolreforminitiative.org/download/tuning-protocol-examining-adult-work

☐ Success Analysis Protocol Examples from the School Reform Initiative:

   • https://schoolreforminitiative.org/doc/success_ana_individuals.pdf

   • http://schoolreforminitiative.org/doc/success_analysis_reflective.pdf

☐
☐
☐
☐

CONCLUSION

You made it. Pause. Breathe deeply.

Recognize that you showed up as a learner for yourself, your team, and your students.

Acknowledge that you made space to reflect on the practices you need to move beyond (or share) as well as those that you might add to strengthen your professional and organizational capacity. The act of true learning is about letting go as much as it is about letting in.

When it came time to determine the title and design the cover for this book, the collaborative effort among my professional network truly became a case study in team learning. It began with a deeply engaging (and very long) lunch with my editor to discuss educators' *real* needs transparently and authentically and what might resonate best with their current reality. This was followed by countless conversations with educators in the field, along with partners working shoulder-to-shoulder with them, to hear and amplify their voices.

After all the dialogue and reflection, two central themes emerged:

1. As educators, we have a responsibility to be constant learners for our students, modeling curiosity, personal and professional growth, and collaboration. But this concept that we are *still learning* should not—and must not—imply that we are always busy and in motion. That notion is irresponsible, promotes burnout, and perpetuates the perception that learning occurs only through constant activity. In contrast, some of the most powerful learning emerges through reflection and stillness. Our commitment to *still learning* as educators is as much about pause as it is about progress. Some of our most meaningful work does not emerge from a flurry of activity but, rather, from time to step back, reflect, and be still.

2. Educators need to be OK with letting go. In the cover design process, I was continually drawn to the image of a dandelion. To some, it might be seen as a weed or a nuisance. To me, it represented the concept of letting go that we struggle with so much as educators—letting go of policies, programs, processes, and everything in between—because we need to "do it all." I took comfort in the assurance that, much like a dandelion, even if we were letting go to make room for new learning, we were still sharing current and past practices with others who might benefit from their integration. The image provided an invitation to simultaneously make space while also sharing our collective experience to promote growth.

In some ways it is the end of this book, but it is really just the beginning. This book was not crafted to be a "one and done" read. In fact, I hope you only read one chapter, or even just a few sections, at a time and put it aside to integrate one of the disciplines or strategies into your practice before coming back to the next. I hope this becomes a perennial read for you as you set annual goals, shift positions, and consider your next professional steps both inside and outside your present organization—whether that is a team, school, or district.

That being said, I imagine there are some readers who hated this text—not because it lacks value, but because the framework it outlines and the action steps it recommends are downright *hard*. While I hope I have empowered you with capacity-building spirit and inspiration for what is possible within education, I recognize this is not a "read and run" type of ed book. It is not one day of educator wellness activities, a quick SEL checklist, or even an annual improvement plan full of SGOs or SLOs (or any number of other educational abbreviations). I have done my best to distill, synthesize, and organize challenging theories and practices to clear reflection questions and action tools to accelerate both individual and organizational growth. There are no Band-Aids, quick fixes, or false recharges in capacity building. It takes a mutual commitment of personal dedication, team understanding, and systems-level change. Writing a Top 10 list, migrating a feel-good keynote from microphone to page, or curating a collection of wellness journal prompts will not get it done. This is the real work, the messy work—and it is also the work that matters. It is our collective heart and soul on the page. But I also hope it is a compass to guide a sustainable path ahead.

If you feel overwhelmed, remember that it is not about *all of the things* but, rather, *the one thing.* Focus and recenter. Keep yourself and one another in the game. You are enough. We—and your students—need you.

APPENDIXES

APPENDIX A: ATTUNEMENT

You can use the QR code or visit https://www.thelearningloop.com/book-attunement to access editable PDF versions of the tools referred to in this appendix. Use the case-sensitive password "StillLearning" to download the resources.

Integration Guide: Attunement

	Harmony Between Perceived Self and Presented Self		
	Perceived Self	**=**	**Presented Self**
Identity Who are you?	*Consider:* Static components: sex, race, ethnicity, national origin, first language Dynamic components: gender, nationality, socioeconomic status, income, sexual orientation, physical/emotional/developmental (dis)ability, age, religious or spiritual affiliation, education, occupation, work experience, organizational role, political ideology, appearance		
Drive What motivates you?	*Consider:* • The hierarchy of professional needs • Expectancy and value • Self-efficacy • Autonomy and personal mastery • Your own personal vision for growth	**Self-Harmony**	**Learning Professional** *Engage in an attunement cycle of experiential learning:* • **Feel**—Concrete experience • **Watch**—Reflection observation • **Think**—Abstract conceptualization • **Do**—Active experimentation
Growth Profile How do you learn and evolve?	*Consider:* • How you respond to inner and outer expectations • Your dominant personality type • Your personality preferences • Your competency strengths • Virtues and human capacities		

Capacity-Building Plan: Attunement

Component	Pause and Reflect	Cultivate Your Capacity	Cultivate Organizational Capacity
Identity	☐ Complete Attunement Reflection: Identity (Figure 1.2, p. 21).	☐ Identify one component of your static or dynamic identity that does not "show up" professionally. ☐ Reflect on why that is. ☐ Identify an action you can take to show up more fully in your school community. ☐ Share action step(s) with an accountability partner.	☐ Identify one area in which it may be difficult for staff members to bring their full selves to school. ☐ Reflect on why that may be. ☐ Identify an action you can take and the resources you will need to support others in showing up more fully in your school community. ☐ Make a plan for how and with whom you will advocate for others.
Drive	☐ Complete Attunement Reflection: Hierarchy of Professional Needs (Figure 1.3, p. 24). ☐ Complete Attunement Reflection: Personal Vision for Growth (Figure 1.4, p. 28).	☐ Identify a tier where you may be stuck. ☐ Select opportunities or experiences that may broaden your perspective. ☐ Identify one opportunity you will actively seek out for continued growth. ☐ Review your personal vision for growth. ☐ Focus on the impact of your efforts and what you are creating. ☐ Identify one step you can take in the next three months. ☐ Share action steps with an accountability partner.	☐ Identify a tier where your team, school, or district may be stuck. ☐ Identify action steps you can recommend or actualize and the resources you will need to effectively implement them. ☐ Make a plan for how and with whom you will advocate. ☐ Provide an opportunity for your team to draft a personal vision for growth. ☐ Encourage team members to share how they envision their future work together. ☐ Describe what their continued collaboration looks like. ☐ Identify ways they can support one another in the next three months, six months, and year to move closer to their vision.

Component	Pause and Reflect	Cultivate Your Capacity	Cultivate Organizational Capacity
Growth Profile	☐ Review the various growth profiles outlined in Chapter 1. ☐ Reflect on which model most aligns to your current personal and professional needs.	☐ Complete at least one of the following assessments and the corresponding "Attunement Discipline in Practice" tools: • Tendencies (Figure 1.5, p. 31) • Enneagram Types (Figure 1.6, p. 33) • Type Indicators (Figure 1.7, p. 36) • Strengths-Based Learning (Figure 1.8, p. 38) • Character Strengths (Figure 1.9, p. 40) ☐ Review the related report(s). ☐ Identify next steps.	☐ Identify which growth profile model best meets staff members' needs. ☐ Facilitate a professional learning opportunity for assessment, analysis, and team discussion. ☐ Outline a plan for continued work and review. ☐ Look for opportunities to integrate growth profiles into staff members' professional growth plans.

APPENDIX B: ALIGNMENT

You can use the QR code or visit https://www.thelearningloop.com/book-alignment to access editable PDF versions of the tools referred to in this appendix. Use the case-sensitive password "StillLearning" to download the resources.

Integration Guide: Alignment

Congruence Between Purpose and Practice

Purpose = Practice

Purpose

Self-Direction

Goals
Who we aim to be

Bucket List
• Circle of Being
• Circle of Relating
• Circle of Doing

The Power of Three

SMARTER Goals
• Specific
• Measurable
• Actionable
• Risky
• Time-Keyed
• Exciting
• Relevant

Practice

Structured Time

Chronotype
• Morning Type
• Evening Type
• Daytime Sleepy Type
• Daytime Type
• Highly Active Type
• Moderately Active Type

Tuning Techniques
• Filter with fences
• Stack time blocks intentionally
• Utilize the Pomodoro method

Time Blocks
• Student Connection
• Focus
• Social
• Administrative
• Recovery
• Personal Connection

Disciplined Action

Habits
• Cue/trigger
• Routine
• Reward

Sticking
• Morning Ritual
• Launch Ritual
• Shutdown Ritual
• Evening Ritual

Stacking
Existing habit performed consistently
→
New goal-aligned habit to stack

Cadence of Accountability

Partner
• Lateral colleague
• Consistent commitment

Playbook
• Account
• Review
• Plan

Pause
• Recenter
• Assess alignment between purpose and practice

Capacity-Building Plan: Alignment

Component	Pause and Reflect	Cultivate Your Capacity	Cultivate Organizational Capacity
Goals	☐ Revisit your personal vision for growth from Chapter 1 (Figure 1.4, p. 28) and reflect on who you want to become. ☐ Complete the Goals Bucket List in Figure 2.2 (p. 52). ☐ Set SMARTER goals (Figure 2.3, p. 55).	☐ Post bucket list in a highly visible location. ☐ Revisit list monthly. ☐ Include three SMARTER goals in your planner. ☐ Revisit these goals weekly. ☐ Use the QR code on page 172 to download and use the quarterly goal sheets provided in the SMARTER Goals Planner.	☐ Facilitate conversations with team members about bucket lists. ☐ Identify ways you can support one another's goal attainment. ☐ Share the SMARTER goals with your team to support one another's goal development. ☐ Inquire about team members' goal progress weekly.
Fresh Starts	☐ Identify at least three social or personal temporal (or time-based) landmarks.	☐ Add temporal landmarks to your planner or calendar. ☐ Match temporal landmarks to bucket list items or SMARTER goals.	☐ Leverage an institutional or site-based shared calendar to highlight possible temporal landmarks for your learning community.
Chronotypes	☐ Identify the chronotype that best matches your energy flow. ☐ Note planning considerations for different times of the day (Figure 2.5, p. 61).	☐ Take an auto-scored or self-scored chronotype assessment to better understand your chronotype.	☐ Ask team members about their chronotypes and sync activities to optimize efficiency and effectiveness.
Time Blocking	☐ Identify time blocks you will use to structure your time (Figure 2.7, p. 69).	☐ Reflect on calendar and planner system(s) and adjust or refine if needed. ☐ Use the QR code on page 172 to download and complete the Model Week Blueprint to help you distinguish among day-to-day variations in your time blocks (beyond just weekday and weekend). ☐ Label or color-code items on task list by time block to focus and optimize each calendar block.	☐ Review master and team schedules to assess whether adjustments need to be made. ☐ Make refinements as able. ☐ Share the Model Week Blueprint template with your team to support their time-blocking practices.

Component	Pause and Reflect	Cultivate Your Capacity	Cultivate Organizational Capacity
Tuning Techniques	☐ Revisit your Goals Bucket List (Figure 2.2, p. 52). ☐ Identify positions or responsibilities you may need to consider letting go of to filter time for goal-oriented tasks. ☐ Revisit your Model Week Blueprint and look for opportunities for intentional stacking. ☐ Consider whether the Pomodoro technique would enhance your workflow.	☐ Plan to let one position or responsibility go per quarter for the next year and add this to your planner. ☐ Update your Model Week Blueprint to integrate intentional stacking where possible and practical. ☐ Download an app to support your application of the Pomodoro technique. ☐ Use the QR code on page 172 to download and utilize the Weekly Planner.	☐ Identify individuals who are overloaded with positions or responsibilities. ☐ Meet with them to reduce these tasks and make a transition plan. ☐ Review master or team schedules to look for opportunities to integrate more intentional stacking. ☐ Check in with team members about focus tools that are working for them and share them widely. ☐ Share the Weekly Planner with your team to provide an additional resource to tune their schedule.
Habits, Stacking, and Sticking	☐ Identify two or three habits directly aligned to three big goals for this quarter. ☐ Identify two or three existing habits you perform consistently that you can leverage as triggers for new habits. ☐ Identify a current (poor) habit you perform consistently and would like to refine or replace.	☐ Craft a consistent ritual (four to eight actions) for at least one segment of the day. Refer to the sample rituals in Figure 2.8 (p. 84). ☐ Add a habit tracker to your planner or download a habit-tracking app. ☐ Use sticky notes to create cues for stacking habits.	☐ Identify organizational habits with potential to increase team performance. ☐ Establish, share, and regularly update team tracker. ☐ Ritualize meetings and/or routines using agenda templates, protocols, note-taking tools, and action plan graphic organizers. ☐ Share the sample rituals in Figure 2.8 with your team to support their individual growth and further refine your team.
Partners, Playbooks, and Pauses	☐ Identify at least two potential accountability partners. ☐ Approach them to gauge their interest. ☐ Consider what you might want your "playbook" to look and sound like. ☐ Reflect on how you will commit to these moments of pause.	☐ Set a time to establish playbook or norms with accountability partner(s). ☐ Consider an agenda or note-taking tools. ☐ Block out meeting times on a calendar.	☐ Offer recommendations for accountability partner pairings. ☐ Provide sample agendas or note-taking tools to guide the process. ☐ Dedicate organizational time (20–30 minutes/week) for accountability partners to connect, reflect, and recommit.

APPENDIX C: PERSPECTIVE

You can use the QR code or visit https://www.thelearningloop.com/book-perspective to access editable PDF versions of the tools referred to in this appendix. Use the case-sensitive password "StillLearning" to download the resources.

Integration Guide: Perspective

Organizationally: **Safety, Belonging, and Vulnerability That Lead to Connected Learning Community**
Individually: **Shift in Schema and Reflection That Leads to Integrated Change in Behavior**

Organizational Commitment	*Organizational Commitment*	*Organizational Outcome*

Build Safety
• Spotlight your fallibility early on.
• Embrace the messenger.
• Make sure everyone has a voice.
• Capitalize on threshold moments.
<div align="right">(Coyle, 2018a)</div>
Foster Belonging
Mentor Types
• Sponsor
• Wing-person
• Cheerleader
• Ally from the "other side"
• Buddy
<div align="right">(Jacob et al., 2020)</div>
	Embolden Vulnerability
	• Be vulnerable first and often.
	• Listen like a trampoline.
	• Nurture candor-generating practices.
	  – After-action reviews
	  – "The Braintrust" and solution groups
	  – Establish boundaries between per-
	    formance reviews and professional
	    learning.
	<div align="right">(Coyle, 2018a)</div>
		Learning Community Connected Through Shared Experience

	=	
Individual Commitment	*Individual Commitment*	*Individual Outcome*
Catalyze a Shift in Schema *Perspective Transformation* • Transmissional: "I see you." • Transactional: "I value you." • Transformational: "I will question/reorder/ shift my thinking or actions." <div align="right">(Brookfield, 2000)</div>	**Make Space for Reflection** • Journaling • Thought partners • Masterminds • Professional learning networks • Accountability relationships • Mindful breathing • Intentional pauses in workflow • Stretching and yoga	**Integrated Change in Behavior**

Capacity-Building Plan: Perspective

Component	Pause and Reflect	Cultivate Your Capacity	Cultivate Organizational Capacity
		Organizational Commitment	
Build Safety	☐ Complete Perspective Reflection: Build Safety (Figure 3.2, p. 100).	☐ Identify one growth opportunity from reflection. ☐ Review next steps and considerations. ☐ Take action to refine practice. ☐ Share action steps with an accountability partner.	☐ Set up "Actions for Building Safe Spaces" as a gallery walk. ☐ Invite staff members to identify individuals who "spotlight fallibility early on" and "embrace the messenger." ☐ Ask staff members how to better leverage the physical environment, mechanisms for input, and threshold moments.
Foster Belonging	☐ Complete Perspective Reflection: Foster Belonging (Figure 3.3, p. 103).	☐ Select one idea for connection from reflection. ☐ Schedule initial mentoring meeting (20–30 minutes) within the next month. ☐ Schedule collaboration meeting (2+ hours) within the next three months. ☐ Set clear outcomes and agenda for collaboration. ☐ Make an action plan following collaboration meeting.	☐ Reflect on how to use the mentor categories in onboarding processes. ☐ Identify staff members you might match now. ☐ Evaluate systems and structures to support future mentoring connections. ☐ Adjust and refine coaching practices to improve the quality of authentic collaboration.
Embolden Vulnerability	☐ Complete Perspective Reflection: Embolden Vulnerability (Figure 3.4, p. 109).	☐ Audio-record a dialogue with a trusted peer. ☐ Transcribe the conversation for reflection. ☐ Note areas where you listened and responded versus amplified. ☐ Identify patterns in responses, reflection points, and transitions. ☐ Note energy-giving practices to be replicated and deflating practices to be avoided.	☐ Video-record a team meeting or gathering. ☐ Set collective norms for communication. ☐ View recording and make note of strengths and growth opportunities. ☐ Encourage team members to view and do the same. ☐ Learn more about after-action reviews and solution groups. ☐ Consider the role(s) they might play in your school community.

Component	Pause and Reflect	Cultivate Your Capacity	Cultivate Organizational Capacity
		Individual Commitment	
Catalyze a Shift in Schema	☐ Reflect on ways you may be "stuck" in your practice (e.g., instructional planning, assessment design, feedback or grading practices). ☐ Identify an area where you want to gain broader perspective and explore a possible shift in mindset or practice.	☐ Collect a classroom-based data set that sets up a disconnect between existing and possible practice. ☐ Use the data to engage in conversation with an accountability partner or team member. ☐ Identify trends and seek possible causes. ☐ Draft 2–3 prompts you will use to capture additional insights. ☐ Meet again to share findings.	☐ Collect a data set that sets up an intentional disconnect between existing and possible practice. ☐ Use protocols to facilitate one-on-one or team conversations. ☐ Embed key action steps into reflection tools to capture evidence of perspective shifts.
Make Space for Reflection	☐ Consider your most gratifying reflection medium (e.g., journaling, thought partner, mastermind, professional learning network, mindful breathing, yoga).	☐ Schedule time daily for reflection. ☐ Experiment with a blank page, different prompts, discussion protocols, guided movements, and so on to find the right balance of structure versus fluidity.	☐ Include reflection as a consistent component of your teams' weekly schedule and professional learning design. ☐ Coach team members in the various forms reflection can take and provide tools and resources as appropriate.

APPENDIX D: COLLECTIVE EFFICACY

You can use the QR code or visit https://www.thelearningloop.com/book-collective-efficacy to access editable PDF versions of the tools referred to in this appendix. Use the case-sensitive password "StillLearning" to download the resources.

Integration Guide: Collective Efficacy

Focus on Continuous Growth to Become a Deliberately Developmental Organization

Trustworthy Community

Shared Vulnerability
- Rank does not have its usual privileges.
- Everyone needs a crew.
- Everyone does people development.
- Everyone builds the culture.
(Kegan & Laskow Lahey, 2016)

Demonstrated Strength
- Compelling data
- Sense of urgency

Continuous Growth

Growth Mindset
- Adults can grow.
- Weakness equals opportunity.

Unifying Focus
- Run on developmental principles.
- Leverage informal mechanisms.
- The bottom line is all one thing.

=

Deliberately Developmental Organization

Capacity-Building Plan: Collective Efficacy

Component	Pause and Reflect	Cultivate Your Capacity	Cultivate Organizational Capacity
Self-Efficacy	☐ Complete the Generalized Self-Efficacy scale (pp. 120–121). ☐ Calculate your total score.	See Chapter 2.	See Chapter 2.
Trustworthy Community: *Shared Vulnerability*	☐ Reflect on a time when you struggled to be professionally vulnerable.	☐ Identify vulnerability gaps within your own professional practice and the organization. ☐ Use the potential gaps list on p. 125 as a guide.	☐ Provide the sentence stems (p. 126) to your team. ☐ Ask them to make a list of what they expect of a trusted leader. ☐ Review the responses for patterns. ☐ Co-create trust-based community norms with your team.
Trustworthy Community: *Demonstrated Strength*	☐ Develop one or two wildly important goals that would make a significant difference in your classroom, school, or community.	☐ Collect baseline data. ☐ Consider lead measures that will have the most impact on progress. ☐ Take notes during the implementation phase. ☐ Share goal(s), data, and lead measures with an accountability partner. ☐ Check in periodically over a two-week period. ☐ Collect and review updated data.	☐ Collect team baseline data. ☐ Consider shared lead measures that will have the most impact on progress. ☐ Take and compare notes during the implementation phase. ☐ Check in periodically over a two-week period. ☐ Collect and review updated data.
Continuous Growth: *Growth Mindset*	☐ Identify your current plateau of adult mental complexity. ☐ Complete the Collective Efficacy Reflection: Growth Mindset (Figure 4.2, p. 132). ☐ Identify a current weakness in your professional practice. ☐ Reframe it as a growth opportunity.	☐ Commit to growth. ☐ Identify actions and inactions working against your commitment. ☐ Name your fears and concerns. ☐ Consider which values or assumptions serve your growth well and which may need to be revisited.	☐ Evaluate your teams' use of meeting time. ☐ Identify opportunities to integrate protocols or learning logs. ☐ Consider how to support your team in demonstrating progress over time.

Component	Pause and Reflect	Cultivate Your Capacity	Cultivate Organizational Capacity
Continuous Growth: *Unifying Focus*	☐ Reflect on the unifying focus, or lack thereof, driving your district, school, or team.	☐ Work with your team to draft principles that drive your shared work. ☐ Ensure they reflect your team's values and accelerate progress toward your goals. ☐ Use these principles as guideposts to facilitate team conversations and provide feedback.	☐ Revisit your district or school vision and mission. ☐ Leverage developmental principles as well as more informal mechanisms such as behaviors, norms, and practices, to move the needle closer to achieving your school's mission.

APPENDIX E: ORGANIZATIONAL LEARNING

You can use the QR code or visit https://www.thelearningloop.com/book-organizational-learning to access editable PDF versions of the tools referred to in this appendix. Use the case-sensitive password "StillLearning" to download the resources.

Integration Guide: Organizational Learning

Sustained Commitment to Evolve and Thrive as a Learning Ecosystem

Learning Ecosystem

Technical Problems

Adaptive Challenges

Generative Opportunities

Focus and Filter Through People and Processes

Personal Mastery

Practice Constructive Destabilization
- Generate creative tension between personal vision and current reality.
- Create more formal growth opportunities.
- Shift positions or teams.
- Embrace complexity.

Shared Vision
- Be compelled by people and their collective vitality, not isolated ideas.
- Strive to accomplish something that matters deeply.
- Inspire active expression of goals.
- Foster passionate commitment, rather than compliance.

Mental Models
- Nurture self-awareness and reflective skills.
- Establish a culture that promotes inquiry.
- Leverage shared language and reflection tools.

Team Learning
- Engage in skillful dialogue and discussion.
- Take innovative and coordinated action by finding flow.
- Accelerate growth with immersive and seamless structures and tools.
- Embed reflective practice (L = P + Q + R).

Systems Thinking
- See interrelationships and patterns of change rather than static snapshots.
- Map your shared vision, including teams and functions.
- Cultivate and sustain a thriving learning ecosystem.

Capacity-Building Plan: Organizational Learning

Component	Pause and Reflect	Cultivate Your Capacity	Cultivate Organizational Capacity
Personal Mastery	☐ Reflect on your own personal mastery. ☐ Assess your current level of creative tension. ☐ Identify evidence of constructive destabilization.	☐ Increase or induce more consistent creative tension. ☐ Seek out constructive destabilization opportunities. ☐ Share opportunities with your team as possible levers for growth.	☐ Reflect on the degree to which intrapersonal attunement and alignment disciplines are positioned within your organization's professional learning model. ☐ Identify opportunities to practice constructive destabilization. ☐ Act on at least one potential opportunity.
Shared Vision	☐ Assess the degree to which your district's or school's vision is truly shared as a reflection of its members' personal visions.	☐ Identify elements of your district's or school's vision that reflect members' personal visions. ☐ Determine which components inspire action and which ones feel generalized, sound like stock language, or lack clarity. ☐ Share your reflections with your accountability partner or team for their perspective and input. ☐ Incorporate their feedback into your vision summary. ☐ Present it to your supervisor for further consideration.	☐ Assess whether your district's or school's vision and mission reflect the strengths and aspirations of your educators. ☐ Determine whether your shared vision actively drives organizational systems and day-to-day operations. ☐ Rewrite, revise, or reinvigorate your vision and mission to provide a clear organizational blueprint that inspires action.
Mental Models	☐ Identify mental models within your organization. ☐ Assess whether mental models are paired with shared language or reflection tools to help norm application.	☐ Identify a mental model that could benefit from common language, clearer definition, or a reflection tool. ☐ Draft a summary or create an artifact that fills this gap. ☐ Share it with your team for feedback and refinement.	☐ Select one mental model that could benefit from refinement. ☐ Select one mental model you will actively discard. ☐ Maintain a proportional relationship between new additions and thoughtful eliminations.

Component	Pause and Reflect	Cultivate Your Capacity	Cultivate Organizational Capacity
Team Learning	☐ Identify your organization's team learning strengths. ☐ Capture "groove" moments when dialogue and collaboration flow. ☐ Note the protocols, preparation processes, note-taking guides, and action-planning tools that amplify team learning.	☐ Identify a "groove" point with the potential to accelerate organizational progress. ☐ Consider how you might reduce friction through dialogue or discussion tools and implementation guides. ☐ Share a draft and pilot it with your team, making note of improvements through consistent practice.	☐ Revisit the concept of teams across your organization. ☐ Reconceive of the notion of teams to produce generative learning opportunities accelerated by flow and guided by structures, protocols, and implementation tools.

REFERENCES

American Association of Colleges for Teacher Education. (2022). *Colleges of education: A national portrait, second edition.* https://aacte.org/resources/research-reports-and-briefs/colleges-of-education-a-national-portraitv2

The Aspen Institute National Commission on Social, Emotional, and Academic Development. (2019). *From a nation at risk to a nation at hope.* Author.

Atkinson, J. W. (1957). Motivational determinants of risk-taking behavior. *Psychological Review, 64*(6, Pt.1), 359–372. https://doi.org/10.1037/h0043445

Bandura, A. (1977). Self-efficacy: Toward a unifying theory of behavioral change. *Psychological Review, 84*(2), 191–215. https://doi.org/10.1037/0033-295x.84.2.191

Bandura, A. (1993). Perceived self-efficacy in cognitive development and functioning. *Educational Psychologist, 28*(2), 117–148. https://doi.org/https://doi.org/10.1207/s15326985ep2802_3

Bandura, A. (1997). *Self-efficacy: The exercise of control.* W. H. Freeman.

Becker, K., Steinberg, H., & Kluge, M. (2016, June). Emil Kraepelin's concepts of the phenomenology and physiology of sleep: The first systematic description of chronotypes. *Sleep Medicine Reviews, 27,* 9–19.

Berg, J., Osher, D., Same, M. R., Nolan, E., Benson, D., & Jacobs, N. (2017). *Identifying, defining, and measuring social and emotional competencies.* American Institutes for Research. www.air.org/sites/default/files/downloads/report/Identifying-Defining-and-Measuring-Social-and-Emotional-Competencies-December-2017-rev.pdf

Betz, N. E., Harmon, L. W., & Borgen, F. H. (1996). The relationships of self-efficacy for the Holland themes to gender, occupational group membership, and vocational interests. *Journal of Counseling Psychology, 43*(1), 90–98. https://doi.org/10.1037/0022-0167.43.1.90

Bramante, F. J., Williams, D., Reed, S., Quarfordt, K., Price, H., Noguera, P., Noddings, N., Moses, M. C., Myles Miller, Pace Marshall, S., Kolbe, L. J., Kohn, L., Kagan, S., Jansen, J., Graham, S., Goodlad, J., Fiske, E. B., Eisner, E., Comer, J., & Cobb, P. (2007). *The learning compact redefined: A call to action*. ASCD Commission on the Whole Child.

Brookfield, S. D. (2000). Transformative learning as ideology critique. In J. Mezirow & Associates (Eds.), *Learning as transformation: Critical perspectives on a theory in progress* (pp. 125–150). Jossey-Bass.

Brown, B. (2012). *Daring greatly: How the courage to be vulnerable transforms the way we live, love, parent, and lead*. Avery.

Carroll, J., Rudolph, J. W., & Hatakenaka, S. (2002, October). Lessons learned from non-medical industries: Root cause analysis as culture change at a chemical plant. *Quality and Safety in Health Care, 11*(3), 266–269.

CASEL. (2019). *SEL trends: Strengthening adult SEL*. https://casel.org/wp-content/uploads/2019/11/SEL-Trends-7-11182019.pdf

CASEL. (2020a). *Frameworks briefs: An examination of K–12 SEL learning competencies/standards in 18 states*. https://casel.org/casel-gateway-examining-kthru12-learning-competencies

CASEL. (2020b). *What is the CASEL Framework?* https://casel.org/fundamentals-of-sel/what-is-the-casel-framework

CASEL. (n.d.). *Focus area 2: Strengthen adult SEL*. CASEL Guide to Schoolwide SEL. https://school-guide.casel.org/focus-area-2/overview

Catmull, E. (2014, March 12). Inside the Pixar Braintrust. *Fast Company*. www.fastcompany.com/3027135/inside-the-pixar-braintrust

Centers for Disease Control and Prevention. (2020, February 10). *Components of the Whole School, Whole Community, Whole Child (WSCC)*. www.cdc.gov/healthyschools/wscc/components.htm

Centers for Disease Control and Prevention and ASCD. (2012). *Whole School, Whole Community, Whole Child (WSCC) model*. www.cdc.gov/healthyschools/wscc

Christensen, L., Gittleson, J., & Smith, M. (2021, April 19). *Intentional learning in practice: A 3x3x3 approach*. McKinsey & Company. www.mckinsey.com/capabilities/people-and-organizational-performance/our-insights/intentional-learning-in-practice-a-3x3x3-approach

Clark, M. C. (1991). *The restructuring of meaning: An analysis of the impact of context on transformational learning* (Doctoral dissertation). University of Georgia.

Coyle, D. (2018a). *The culture code: The secrets of highly successful groups*. Bantam Books.

Coyle, D. (2018b, February 20). How showing vulnerability helps build a stronger team. *TED: Ideas Worth Spreading*. https://ideas.ted.com/how-showing-vulnerability-helps-build-a-stronger-team

Cramer, P. (2004). Identity change in adulthood: The contribution of defense mechanisms and life experiences. *Journal of Research in Personality, 38*(3), 280–316. https://doi.org/10.1016/s0092-6566(03)00070-9

Csikszentmihalyi, M. (1990). *Flow: The psychology of optimal experience*. Harper Perennial.

Darling, M., Parry, C., & Moore, J. (2005 , July–August). Learning in the thick of it. *Harvard Business Review*. https://hbr.org/2005/07/learning-in-the-thick-of-it

Dockrill, P. (2020, December 2). There are six human chronotypes, not just morning larks and night owls, study says. *Science Alert*. www.sciencealert.com/scientists-say-there-are-6-human-chronotypes-not-just-morning-people-and-night-owls

Duhigg, C. (2014). *The power of habit: Why we do what we do in life and business*. Random House.

Dweck, C. S. (2006). *Mindset: The new psychology of success*. Ballantine Books.

Eccles, J., Adler, T. F., Futterman, R., Goff, S. B., Kaczala, C. M., Meece, J., & Midgley, C. (1983). Expectancies, values and academic behaviors. In J. T. Spence (Ed.), *Achievement and achievement motives: Psychological and sociological approaches*. W. H. Freeman.

Eells, R. (2011). *Meta-analysis of the relationship between collective efficacy and student achievement* [Published doctoral dissertation]. Loyola University.

Elias, M. J., Zins, J. E., Weissberg, R. P., Frey, K. S., Greenberg, M. T., Haynes, N. M., Kessler, R., Schwab-Stone, M. E., & Shriver, T. P. (1997). *Promoting social and emotional learning: Guidelines for educators*. ASCD.

The Enneagram Institute. (n.d.). *The nine Enneagram type descriptions*. Author. www.enneagramin-stitute.com/type-descriptions

Erikson, E. H. (1968). *Identity: Youth and crisis*. Norton.

Fadjukoff, P., Pulkkinen, L., & Kokko, K. (2016). Identity formation in adulthood: A longitudinal study from age 27 to 50. *Identity, 16*(1), 8–23. https://doi.org/10.1080/15283488.2015.1121820

Fleming, A. (2016, October). The key to adaptable companies is relentlessly developing people. *Harvard Business Review*. https://hbr.org/2016/10/the-key-to-adaptable-companies-is-relentlessly-developing-people

Gallup. (2022, May 26). *Learn about the history of CliftonStrengths*. www.gallup.com/cliftonstrengths/en/253754/history-cliftonstrengths.aspx

Gardner, H. (1983). *Frames of mind: The theory of multiple intelligences*. Basic Books.

Gardner, H. (2006). *Five minds for the future*. Harvard Business School Press.

Gardner, B., Lally, P., & Wardle, J. (2012). Making health habitual: The psychology of "habit-formation" and general practice. *British Journal of General Practice, 62*(605), 664–666. https://doi.org/10.3399/bjgp12x659466

Gilkey, C. (2019). *Start finishing: How to go from idea to done*. Sounds True.

Hair, E. C., Jager, J., & Garrett, S. B. (2002). *Research brief: Helping teens develop healthy social skills and relationships: What the research shows about navigating adolescence*. Child Trends. https://cms.childtrends.org/wp-content/uploads/2002/07/Child_Trends-2002_07_01_RB_TeenSocial Skills.pdf

Hargreaves, A., & Fullan, M. (2012). *Professional capital: Transforming teaching in every school*. Teachers College Press.

Hattie, J. (2016, July). *Mindframes and maximizers: Conference program*. Visible Learning Plus Annual Conference 2016, Washington, DC. Corwin.

Hattie, J. (2018). *Collective teacher efficacy according to John Hattie*. Visible Learning. https://visible-learning.org/2018/03/collective-teacher-efficacy-hattie

Heifetz, R., Grashow, A., & Linsky, M. (2009). *The practice of adaptive leadership: Tools and tactics for changing your organization and the world*. Harvard University Press.

Heifetz, R. A., & Laurie, D. L. (1997, January–February). The work of leadership. *Harvard Business Review, 75*(1), 124–134.

Hite, S. A., & Donohoo, J. (2021). *Leading collective efficacy: Powerful stories of achievement and equity*. Corwin.

Human, L. J., Biesanz, J. C., Parisotto, K. L., & Dunn, E. W. (2012). Your best self helps reveal your true self: Positive self-presentation leads to more accurate personality impressions. *Social Psychological and Personal Science, 3*(1), 23–30. https://journals.sagepub.com/doi/10.1177/1948550611407689

Hunter, E. M., & Wu, C. (2016). Give me a break: Choosing workday break activities to maximize resource recovery. *Journal of Applied Psychology, 101*(2), 302–311.

Hyatt, M. (2019). *Free to focus: A total productivity system to achieve more by doing less.* Baker Books.

Hyatt, M. (2020, March 6). *The beginner's guide to goal setting.* Michael Hyatt & Company. https://michaelhyatt.com/goal-setting

Hyatt, M., & Harkavy, D. (2016). *Living forward: A proven plan to stop drifting and get the life you want.* Baker Books.

Ingersoll, R. M., Merrill, L., Stuckey, D., & Collins, G. (2018). Seven trends: The transformation of the teaching force. *CPRE Research Reports.* https://repository.upenn.edu/entities/publication/f179131d-02df-47a7-b24d-0201ce0521e5

Ingersoll, R. M., Sirinides, P., & Dougherty, P. (2017). School leadership, teachers' roles in school decision making, and student achievement. *CPRE Working Papers.* https://repository.upenn.edu/cpre_workingpapers/15

Jacob, K., Unerman, S., & Edwards, M. (2020). *Belonging: The key to transforming and maintaining diversity, inclusion, and equality at work.* Bloomsbury.

Jones, S. M., Bailey, R., & Nelson, B. (2018, December). *Compare skill focus across frameworks.* Explore SEL. http://exploresel.gse.harvard.edu/compare-domains

Jones, S. M., & Kahn, J. (2017–2018). The evidence base for how learning happens: A consensus on social, emotional, and academic development. *American Educator,* 16–21.

Josselson, R. (1996). *Revising herself: The story of women's identity from college to midlife.* Oxford University Press.

Katz, S., Earl, L. M., & Ben Jaafar, S. (2009). *Building and connecting learning communities: The power of networks for school improvement.* Corwin.

Kegan, R., & Laskow Lahey, L. (2016). *An everyone culture: Becoming a deliberately developmental organization.* Harvard Business School Publishing.

Kim, M., & Shin, Y. (2015). Collective efficacy as a mediator between cooperative group norms and group positive affect and team creativity. *Asia Pacific Journal of Management, 32*(3). https://doi.org/10.1007/s10490-015-9413-4

Knowles, M. S., Holton, E. F., & Swanson, R. A. (2005). *The adult learner: The definitive classic in adult education and human resource development* (6th ed.). Elsevier.

Kolb, D. A., & Fry, R. E. (1974). *Toward an applied theory of experiential learning.* MIT Alfred P. Sloan School of Management.

Kroger, J., Martinussen, M., & Marcia, J. E. (2010). Identity status change during adolescence and young adulthood: A meta-analysis. *Journal of Adolescence, 33*(5), 683–698. https://doi.org/10.1016/j.adolescence.2009.11.002

Kruger, J., & Dunning, D. (1999). Unskilled and unaware of it: How difficulties in recognizing one's own incompetence lead to inflated self-assessments. *Journal of Personality and Social Psychology, 77*(6), 1121–1134. https://doi.org/10.1037//0022-3514.77.6.1121

Locke, E. A., & Latham, G. P. (2013). *New developments in goal setting and task performance.* Routledge.

Maddux, J. E. (Ed.). (2013). *Self-efficacy, adaptation, and adjustment: Theory, research, and application.* Springer Science & Business Media.

Marquardt, M., Leonard, H. S., Freedman, A., & Hill, C. (2009). *Action learning for developing leaders and organizations: Principles, strategies, and cases.* American Psychological Association.

Maslow, A. H. (1943). A theory of human motivation. *Psychological Review, 50*(4), 370–396. https://doi.org/10.1037/h0054346

McChesney, C., Covey, S., & Huling, J. (2016). *The 4 disciplines of execution: Achieving your wildly important goals.* Free Press.

Mezirow, J. (1978). Perspective transformation. *Adult Education, 28*(2), 100–110. https://doi.org/10.1177/074171367802800202

Mezirow, J. (1991). *Transformative dimensions of adult learning.* Jossey-Bass.

Mezirow, J. (1995). Transformation theory of adult learning. In M. R. Welton (Ed.), *In defense of the lifeworld* (pp. 39–70). SUNY Press.

The Myers-Briggs Company. (n.d.). *What is MBTI and why use it?* MBTIonline. www.mbtionline.com/en-US/How-it-works/Framework

National Center for Education Statistics. (2020). Highlights of U.S. PISA 2018 results web report (NCES 2020-166 and NCES 2020-072). U.S. Department of Education. Institute of Education Sciences, National Center for Education Statistics. https://nces.ed.gov/surveys/pisa/pisa2018

Network for College Success. (n.d.). *Tool set B: Unpacking adult mindsets.* University of Chicago, Crown Family School of Social Work, Policy, and Practice.

O'Brien, W. (2006). *Character and the corporation.* Society for Organizational Learning.

OECD. (2022). *Education at a glance 2022: OECD indicators.* OECD Publishing. https://doi.org/10.1787/3197152b-en

Putilov, A. A., Marcoen, N., Neu, D., Pattyn, N., & Mairesse, O. (2019). There is more to chronotypes than evening and morning types: Results of a large-scale community survey provide evidence for high prevalence of two further types. *Personality and Individual Difference, 148,* 77–84.

Putilov, A. A., Sveshnikov, D. S., Puchkova, A. N., Dorokhov, V. B., Bakaeva, Z. B., Yakunina, E. B., Starshinov, Y. P., Torshin, V. I., Alipov, N. N., Sergeeva, O. V., Trutneva, E. A., Lapkin, M. M., Lopatskaya, Z. N., Budkevich, R. O., Budkevich, E. V., Dyakovich, M. P., Donskaya, O. G., Plusnin, J. M., Delwiche, B., Colomb, C., et al. (2021). Single-item chronotyping (SIC), a method to self-assess diurnal types by using six simple charts. *Personality and Individual Differences, 168.* https://doi.org/https://doi.org/10.1016/j.paid.2020.110353

Quaglia, R. J., & Lande, L. L. (2017). *Teacher voice: Amplifying success.* Corwin.

Revans, R. (1982). *The origins and growth of action learning.* Krieger.

Revans, R. (1983). Action learning: Its origins and nature. In M. Pedler (Ed.), *Action learning in practice.* Gower.

Rodman, A. (2019). *Personalized professional learning: A job-embedded pathway for elevating teacher voice.* ASCD.

Rodman, A., Farias, A., & Szymczak, S. (2020). When Netflix isn't enough: Fostering true recovery for educators. *Educational Leadership, 78*(4). www.ascd.org/el/articles/when-netflix-isnt-enough-fostering-true-recovery-for-educators

Rodman, A., & Thompson, J. (2019, July). Eight things teams do to sabotage their work. *Educational Leadership, 76*(9). www.ascd.org/el/articles/eight-things-teams-do-to-sabotage-their-work

Roenneberg, T., Wirz-Justice, A., & Merrow, M. (2003, February). Life between clocks: Daily temporal patterns of human chronotypes. *Journal of Biological Rhythms, 18*(1), 80–90.

Rubin, G. (2018). *The four tendencies: The indispensable personality profiles that reveal how to make your life better (and other people's lives better, too).* Two Roads.

Sampson, R. J., Raudenbush, S. W., & Earls, F. (1997). Neighborhoods and violent crime: A multilevel study of collective efficacy. *Science, 277*(5328), 918–924. https://doi.org/10.1126/science.277.5328.918

Saphier, J. (2019). *The "black box" of collective efficacy.* Research for Better Teaching.

Schleicher, A. (2019). *PISA 2018: Insights and interpretations.* Organisation for Economic Co-operation and Development.

Scholz, U., Doña, B. G., Sud, S., & Schwarzer, R. (2002). Is general self-efficacy a universal construct? Psychometric findings from 25 countries. *European Journal of Psychological Assessment, 18*(3), 242–251. https://psycnet.apa.org/record/2002-06643-007

Schwartz, K. (2020, January 26). Why focusing on adult learning builds a school culture where students thrive. *MindShift*. www.kqed.org/mindshift/54750/why-focusing-on-adult-learning-builds-a-school-culture-where-students-thrive

Schwarzer, R., & Jersusalem, M. (1995). Generalized self-efficacy scale. In J. Weinman, S. Wright, & M. Johnston (Eds.), *Measures in health psychology: A user's portfolio* (pp. 35–37). NFER-Nelson.

Senge, P. M. (2006). *The fifth discipline: The art and practice of the learning organization*. Random House Business.

Senge, P. M., Cambron-McCabe, N., Lucas, T., Smith, B., Dutton, J., & Kleiner, A. (2000). *Schools that learn: A fifth discipline fieldbook for educators, parents, and everyone who cares about education*. Currency.

Slade, S. (2020, January/February). It's time for a whole-child movement. *AC&E/Equity & Access*. www.ace-ed.org/its-time-for-a-whole-child-movement

Sussex Publishers. (n.d.). Bias. *Psychology Today*. www.psychologytoday.com/us/basics/bias

Taylor, E. W. (1998). *The theory and practice of transformative learning: A critical review* (Ser. 374). ERIC Clearinghouse on Adult, Career, and Vocational Education, Center on Education and Training for Employment, College of Education, Ohio State University.

United Nations. (n.d.). Capacity-building. *Academic Impact*. www.un.org/en/academic-impact/capacity-building

Vanderkam, L. (2011). *168 Hours: You have more time than you think*. Penguin.

Weick, K. E. (1995). *Sensemaking in organizations*. Sage.

Wigfield, A., & Eccles, J. S. (1992). The development of achievement task values: A theoretical analysis. *Developmental Review, 12*(3), 265–310.

Wiggins, G., & McTighe, J. (2007). *Schooling by design: Mission, action, and achievement*. ASCD.

Zenger, J., & Folkman, J. (2016, July 14). What great listeners actually do. *Harvard Business Review*. https://hbr.org/2016/07/what-great-listeners-actually-do

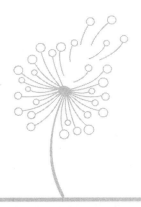

INDEX

The letter *f* following a page number denotes a figure.

ABOUT THE AUTHOR

Allison Rodman is the Founder and Chief Learning Officer of The Learning Loop, an education consulting organization that provides professional learning services to districts, schools, nonprofit organizations, and businesses worldwide. This includes work with public, charter, and independent schools; more than 20 archdioceses; and more than 60 sites across the Americas, Europe, and the Pacific for the Department of Defense Education Activity (DoDEA).

Allison's work focuses on adult learners. She is an ASCD Faculty Member and author of the ASCD book *Personalized Professional Learning: A Job-Embedded Pathway for Elevating Teacher Voice* (2019). She has also written for *Educational Leadership* on professional learning, effective teams, and educator wellness as well as for *Education Week*'s "Classroom Q&A" and *Edutopia*.

Allison has been a pre-conference, concurrent, and featured speaker for ASCD's conferences as well as a pre-conference and concurrent speaker for Learning Forward and a keynote speaker for many state affiliates. She brings experience as a teacher, instructional coach, school leader, director of teaching and learning, director of professional learning, board member, and consultant. Allison received a BA from the University of Richmond (VA), where she majored in Political Science and Secondary Education, and an MSE from the University of Pennsylvania with a concentration in Educational Leadership. She holds certifications as a teacher, principal, board member, master board member, and board leader.

Allison designs, facilitates, and coaches professional learning that is personalized, purposeful, and paradigm-shifting. She is deeply committed to connecting learners and sharing resources to personalize the learning process at every level of the system. The goal of her work is to help adult learners view learning as an ongoing experience (not an endpoint or one-time workshop), strengthen their professional and organizational capacity, and create deliberately developmental organizations. When working with districts and schools, Allison challenges them to examine all aspects of their learning organization and focus on the connections among culture, collaboration, and communication as levers for growth. She encourages and facilitates the design of a personalized, purposeful, and paradigm-shifting approach to professional learning rather than one-time, "sit-and-get" professional development sessions.

Allison's varied experiences enable her to support schools as learning organizations through a variety of different lenses. You can learn more about her work at www.thelearningloop.com and connect with her at arodman@ thelearningloop.com or on social media @thelearningloop.

Related ASCD Resources

At the time of publication, the following resources were available (ASCD stock numbers appear in parentheses).

C.R.A.F.T. Conversations for Teacher Growth: How to Build Bridges and Cultivate Expertise by Sally J. Zepeda, Lakesha Robinson Goff, and Stefanie W. Steele (#120001)

Creating a Culture of Reflective Practice: Capacity-Building for Schoolwide Success by Pete Hall and Alisa A. Simeral (#117006)

Educator Bandwidth: How to Reclaim Your Energy, Passion, and Time by Jane Kise and Ann Holm (#122019)

Facilitating Teacher Teams and Authentic PLCs: The Human Side of Leading People, Protocols, and Practices by Daniel R. Venables (#117004)

Highly Effective PLCs and Teacher Teams (Quick Reference Guide for Leaders) by Steve Ventura and Michelle Ventura (#QRG123050)

Illuminate the Way: The School Leader's Guide to Addressing and Preventing Teacher Burnout by Chase Mielke (#123032)

It's Time for Strategic Scheduling: How to Design Smarter K–12 Schedules That Are Great for Students, Staff, and the Budget by Nathan Levenson and David James (#123019)

Make Teaching Sustainable: Six Shifts That Teachers Want and Students Need by Paul Emerich France (#123011)

The Minimalist Teacher by Tamera Musiowsky-Borneman and C. Y. Arnold (#121058)

Personalized Professional Learning: A Job-Embedded Pathway for Elevating Teacher Voice by Allison Rodman (#118028)

Protocols for Professional Learning (e-book) by Lois Brown Easton (#109037E4)

Schooling by Design: Mission, Action, and Achievement (e-book) by Grant Wiggins and Jay McTighe (#107018E4)

Small Shifts, Meaningful Improvement: Collective Leadership Strategies for Schools and Districts by P. Ann Byrd, Alesha Daughtrey, Jonathan Eckert, and Lori Nazareno (#123007)

Stop Leading, Start Building: Turn Your School into a Success Story with the People and Resources You Already Have by Robyn R. Jackson (#121025)

For up-to-date information about ASCD resources, go to **www.ascd.org.** You can search the complete archives of *Educational Leadership* at **www.ascd.org/el.**

ASCD myTeachSource®
Download resources from a professional learning platform with hundreds of research-based best practices and tools for your classroom at http://myteachsource.ascd.org/.

For more information, send an email to member@ascd.org; call 1-800-933-2723 or 703-578-9600; send a fax to 703-575-5400; or write to Information Services, ASCD, 2800 Shirlington Road, Suite 1001, Arlington, VA 22206 USA.

WHOLE CHILD
TENETS

1 **HEALTHY**
Each student enters school healthy and learns about and practices a healthy lifestyle.

2 **SAFE**
Each student learns in an environment that is physically and emotionally safe for students and adults.

3 **ENGAGED**
Each student is actively engaged in learning and is connected to the school and broader community.

4 **SUPPORTED**
Each student has access to personalized learning and is supported by qualified, caring adults.

5 **CHALLENGED**
Each student is challenged academically and prepared for success in college or further study and for employment and participation in a global environment.

ascd
whole child

The ASCD Whole Child approach is an effort to transition from a focus on narrowly defined academic achievement to one that promotes the long-term development and success of all children. Through this approach, ASCD supports educators, families, community members, and policymakers as they move from a vision about educating the whole child to sustainable, collaborative actions.

Still Learning relates to the **supported** tenet.

For more about the ASCD Whole Child approach, visit www.ascd.org/wholechild.

Become an ASCD member today!
Go to www.ascd.org/joinascd
or call toll-free: 800-933-ASCD (2723)

DON'T MISS A SINGLE ISSUE OF ASCD'S AWARD-WINNING MAGAZINE.

ascd educational leadership

If you belong to a Professional Learning Community, you may be looking for a way to get your fellow educators' minds around a complex topic. Why not delve into a relevant theme issue of *Educational Leadership*, the journal written by educators for educators?

Subscribe now, or purchase back issues of ASCD's flagship publication at **www.ascd.org/el**. Discounts on bulk purchases are available.

To see more details about these and other popular issues of *Educational Leadership*, visit **www.ascd.org/el/all**.

2800 Shirlington Road
Suite 1001
Arlington, VA 22206 USA

www.ascd.org/learnmore